M.S. GOLWALKAR, THE RSS AND INDIA

Jyotirmaya Sharma is professor of political science at the University of Hyderabad. His publications include *Hindutva: Exploring the Idea of Hindu Nationalism*, *A Restatement of Religion: Swami Vivekananda and the Making of Hindu Nationalism*, *Elusive Non-violence* (all published by Context), *The Ocean of Mirth* (Routledge) and an edited volume titled *Grounding Morality: Freedom, Knowledge and the Plurality of Cultures* (co-edited with A. Raghuramaraju). He has been a visiting fellow and lecturer at many prestigious universities and research centres, both in India and abroad. He has also held senior editorial positions at *The Times of India* and *The Hindu* from 1998 to 2006, and continues to write occasional columns.

PRAISE FOR THE BOOK

'The book does mark a refreshing departure from both the strident depiction of Golwalkar as a prototype fascist by secularists as well as the fawning hosannas of the Hindutva bandwagon.'

—Ajoy Bose

'Overall, this is a useful monograph, as there are few studies of Golwalkar.'

—Swapan Dasgupta

'Sharma points out that notwithstanding Golwalkar's fierce adherence to the un-indebted notion of the "Bharatiya", his idea of Hinduism, his notions of self, society, politics and nationalism owe themselves to European Orientalism, Romanticism and Enlightenment. This, in fact, pulls the rug from under the feet of pompous Hindutva. ... [The book] is presented by Jyotirmaya Sharma in quiet, assuring prose. It is a splendid piece of condensation of the writings of the chief ideologue of the RSS, and is done clinically, without raising blood-pressure ...'

—B. Surendara Rao

'... an unusual book that addresses Golwalkar's thought and examines his vision ... of what it meant to be a Hindu.'

—*The Economic Times*

'[Sharma] focuses on examining, carefully and critically, Golwalkar's thoughts and ideas. In the process, he also reveals the hidden dangers, distortions and intellectual vacuity that have gone into the making of Hindu nationalist thinking. ... [He] provides rare glimpses into Golwalkar's persona. ... [He] is convincing when he points out Golwalkar's almost fascist bearings or the lack of originality in his arguments. Sharma also unmasks the malevolent nature of Hindutva, which, he writes, has distorted the true meaning of concepts such as Hinduism and the nation state.'

—*The Telegraph*

M.S. GOLWALKAR, THE RSS AND INDIA

JYOTIRMAYA SHARMA

First published as *Terrifying Vision: M.S. Golwalkar, the RSS and India* by Penguin Books India (Viking) in 2007

Published by Context, an imprint of Westland Books, a division of Nasadiya Technologies Private Limited, in 2023

No. 269/2B, First Floor, 'Irai Arul', Vimalraj Street, Nethaji Nagar, Allappakkam Main Road, Maduravoyal, Chennai 600095

Westland, the Westland logo, Context and the Context logo are the trademarks of Nasadiya Technologies Private Limited, or its affiliates.

ISBN: 9789395767699

10 9 8 7 6 5 4 3 2 1

Typeset in Linux Libertine by Jojy Philip, New Delhi 110015

Printed at Manipal Technologies Limited, Manipal

For Jahnavi

Contents

Introduction

Do Not Forget Me

The Rashtriya Swayamsevak Sangh (RSS; henceforth referred to as Sangh in the book) held a grand public event in Nagpur on 24 February 2006 to commemorate the birth centenary of Madhav Sadashiv Golwalkar. The choice of the date was according to the Hindu lunar calendar. Golwalkar came into this world a few days earlier, on Monday, 19 February 1906, at 4.34 a.m., which was Magha Vadya 11, Shaka 1827 according to the Hindu calendar.[1] He was born into a Karhada Brahmin family in Nagpur. His father, Sadashivrao, was a civil servant who eventually retired as the headmaster of a school. Golwalkar's original surname was Padhye and belonged to Golwali in Konkan.

Sadashivrao wanted him to be a doctor, but Golwalkar had to leave Fergusson College because of some rule that had to do with domicile. He studied science in Nagpur at the Hislop College. After passing his intermediate examination in 1924 with merit, he joined the Banaras Hindu University (BHU), where he received a B.Sc degree in 1926 and an M.Sc in 1928 in zoology in first class. He decided to work on his doctoral thesis at the Marine Aquarium in Madras, but abandoned it after a year due to his father's retirement and the financial difficulties that the family was facing at the time. He was appointed as lecturer in zoology at BHU and worked there between 1930 and 1933. After that, he returned to Nagpur and completed a degree in law in 1935.

Bhayyaji Dani, then a senior Sangh functionary, had established a *shakha* at BHU in 1928. Golwalkar was a frequent visitor there. He first met the Sangh's founder, Dr K.B. Hedgewar, in Banaras in 1931, and subsequently, Hedgewar invited him to Nagpur in 1932 to attend the annual Vijayadashmi function. He was appointed the *karyavah* or secretary of the main branch of the Sangh in 1934. Between 1937 and 1939, he held charge of the Officers' Training Camp at Nagpur, considered a very important office within the Sangh. In 1939, he was made the *sarkaryawaha* or general secretary of the Sangh, the second most important position within the Sangh. After Hedgewar's death in 1940, Golwalkar was appointed *sarsanghchalak* or supreme guide of the Sangh, an office he held for thirty-three years, until his death in June 1973. He was imprisoned, and his organization banned, after Gandhi's assassination. Except for this brief interruption in his Sangh related activities between February 1948 and July 1949, his life after 1940 was indistinguishable from that of the Sangh.[2]

There are few sharp turns and dramatic moments in Golwalkar's life. One event that stands out is his sudden decision to abandon his legal practice and the Sangh's work and go to Swami Akhandananda for spiritual initiation. Golwalkar was close to Swami Bhaskareshwarananda of the Ramakrishna Mission in the Dhamtoli area of Nagpur. He was also encouraged by Swami Amoortananda, known as Amitabh Maharaj, to seek spiritual guidance from Swami Akhandananda. He left for Sargachhi in 1936 without telling anyone, and his guru gave him *deeksha* or initiation on 13 January 1937. Akhandananda died on 7 February 1937, and towards the end of March 1937, Golwalkar returned to Nagpur.

Golwalkar's association with Swami Akhandananda was decisive in two significant ways. Akhandananda was Ramakrishna Paramahansa's direct disciple and Swami Vivekananda's *guru bhai* or fellow disciple. From him, Golwalkar inherited the nationalist legacy of Vivekananda. Akhandananda also passed on to Golwalkar his ideal of *seva* or service as a way of uniting Hindus. However, as Gwilym Beckerlegge has pointed out, Akhandananda's credo of service to humanity was even prior to that of Vivekananda, but it lacked elements of any negative critique of Hinduism and attempts at revitalization of Hinduism that are popularly, and somewhat exaggeratedly, attributed to Vivekananda.[3]

A few quotes from Akhandananda would help illustrate the manner in which Golwalkar inherited the Vivekananda–Akhandananda legacy. In the context of service, Akhandananda says:

> Renunciation of one's own interest, and service as if to one's own self – not showing kindness to 'others' – this is Karmayoga, this is sevadharma, the religion of service ... By serving, the heart is purified; by serving, the heart expands; by such service one can see oneself in all.[4]

The service of humanity soon translates into a close association with the nation:

> Swamiji's [Swami Vivekananda] 'love' for the country is not so easy to understand. It is not 'patriotism'; it is identification of the Self with the country (deśātma-bodh). Ordinary people identify the Self with the body (dehātma-bodh); so they are always mad after the happiness and comfort of the body. But

> in the case of Swamiji, he was absorbed in the thought of the country and his countrymen – their past, present and future. That is not all. There is a stage beyond this: identification with all (viśvātma-bodh), thinking of the good of all.[5]

To reiterate what has been said above, Golwalkar was the 'inheritor' of the Vivekananda–Akhandananda legacy. Beckerlegge calls this an instance of 'appropriation'.[6] It is, however, safe to conclude that this legacy is now a part of the geneology of ideas represented by Hindutva and its politics.[7]

There is scant material on the personal aspects of Golwalkar's life. Letters written to Baburao Telang in 1929 and to Vamanrao Deshpande in 1931 provide a small but significant glimpse into a few personal facets. In a letter to Telang he describes himself as a person of independent spirit and 'the angry son of a short-tempered father'.[8] He speaks of the 'pure blood [that] flows in every vein of mine'.[9] He tells Telang of an illness, during which he started smoking in order to amuse himself. He also speaks of the agony involved in eating an egg every day to regain health. Writing to Telang on 28 February 1929, he confesses to his fear of moving towards some kind of decadence or even romance.[10] In another exchange, he expresses his admiration for *Uncle Tom's Cabin*, calling it excellent, moving, and a novel full of merits.[11]

Again writing to Telang on 16 March 1929, the young Golwalkar provides an interesting list of his own strengths and virtues.[12] It reads as follows:

1. Malkhamb champion;
2. Expert in war; used his hands in the Nagpur riots;
3. A votary of Hindu pride;
4. Politician;

5. Grahastashrami or householder. (Before listing his virtues, Golwalkar says to Telang that he wanted to be a householder without the mistress of the house. Now, while compiling the list, he quotes Milton: 'The only bliss of paradise which has survived its fall'.)
6. Old despite being young;
7. Selfless;
8. Metaphysician.

As he grew older and assumed the responsibilities of the Sangh, he perceived his *karma* as being tied to the Sangh. But he often despaired of exhaustion and bad health. In a rare display of resignation, he writes to M.N. Ghatate of Nasik on 2 June 1954: 'I am crumbling now. Why have attachment to a crumbling structure?'[13] The memories of his time in Sargachhi with Swami Akhandananda often moved and agitated him.[14] Another rare display of emotion came with the death of his mother in 1961.[15] In the third letter that he wrote as part of his last will and testament on 2 April 1973 (this was opened after his death on 6 June 1973), he apologized 'with folded hands' for hurting anyone due to 'my nature or other inadequacies'.[16] Quoting Tukaram, he prayed that he ought not to be forgotten by God and by men of virtue.

Though Golwalkar was not the founder of the RSS, he cast the organization in his own image and remains to this day its most influential ideologue. He gave direction to the Sangh for thirty-three long years. The growth of the Sangh and that of the 'inspired' organizations of the Sangh Parivar is the result of his vision of Hindu consolidation.

Golwalkar wrote a great deal, gave interviews, answered letters and lectured extensively in his capacity as *sarsanghchalak* or the Sangh's chief mentor. Yet, popular perception reduces his oeuvre to just two books: *Bunch of Thoughts* and *We or Our Nationhood Defined.*[17] Of these two, Golwalkar did not write *We or Our Nationhood Defined,* though he controversially appended his name to it.[18] It has now been formally withdrawn. In 2005, the Dr. Hedgewar Smarak Samiti published Golwalkar's complete works in twelve volumes.[19] Golwalkar's speeches, articles and letters are variously in Hindi, Marathi and English, though he advocated and preferred Hindi. There are a few letters written to scholars in Sanskrit as well. This set updates and completes the rather inadequate material available in an earlier seven-volume attempt, which was titled *Shri Guruji Samagra Darshan.*[20] It equips us to go beyond the limitations posed by an excessive reliance on *Bunch of Thoughts* as representative of Golwalkar's thought. It must also be said that very little changed in Golwalkar's thought in the three decades and more that he led the Sangh. There were no major breaks, departures, rupture or re-evaluation in the ideas he held dear and propagated for achieving his utopia of a Hindu Rashtra.

Above all, a compelling reason for writing this book is to examine the thought that so decisively influenced politics in India in the 1980s and the 1990s. The Ramjanmabhoomi movement, the demolition of the Babri Masjid and the Gujarat riots of 2002 are just a few examples of the impact Golwalkar's legacy has had in the move towards a certain brand of radical Hindu nationalism. Article 4(c) of the Sangh's constitution states that it is 'aloof from politics and is devoted to social and cultural fields only'.[21] Despite the disclaimer, its 'inspired'[22] organizations like the Bharatiya Janata Party (BJP), the Vishva Hindu Parishad (VHP) and the Bajarang Dal, among others, have had a malefic influence on Indian politics in the last three decades. Moreover, these outfits continue to look to the Sangh for ideological inspiration and direction, and the Sangh's role in controlling them goes beyond its professed aim of welding 'together the various groups within the Hindu Samaj and to revitalise and rejuvenate the same on the basis of its Dharma and its Sanskriti'.[23]

There are those who detect dark and diabolical motives in the Sangh's constant distancing of itself from politics. For them, the Sangh intervenes in politics through its affiliates without having to enter the democratic realm. This form of politics by proxy enables it to remain beyond the pale of public scrutiny and accountability.

There are compelling reasons to believe in the schizophrenic tendencies the Sangh and its affiliates often exhibit. It would, however, be useful to ask whether there is an essential schism between our conventional understanding of politics and the Sangh's ideological universe. Even a cursory examination of Golwalkar's thought reveals a profound semantic and conceptual disjuncture between conventional liberal democratic notions of the political and Golwalkar's vision of a Hindu Rashtra or Hindu nation. This view is not entirely incorrect.

A closer look at Golwalkar's ideas, however, unravels three important strands. Firstly, his idea of Hinduism comes from an uncritical acceptance of the way European orientalists[24] had sought to define it in the eighteenth and nineteenth centuries. Secondly, his conceptions of self, society and politics were entirely borrowed from trends current in European thought since the eighteenth century. Thirdly, his vision of a Hindu Rashtra and his shaping of the Sangh owed more to certain ideas of European Enlightenment, nationalism and romanticism than is normally acknowledged. In other words, there is nothing Hindu or Bharatiya in Golwalkar's entire ideological universe.[25] This is the supreme irony in Golwalkar's thought. His attempts at Hindu consolidation and his dream of reinstating a Hindu Rashtra were, in the end, someone else's project. Establishing this is the third, and most compelling reason, for writing this book.

—

It was as late as 1986 that a group of scholars met at Wilhelmsfeld in Heidelberg to reconsider Hinduism.[26] Two major approaches to the study of Hinduism emerged out of this conclave. The first was an attempt to construct a unity within Hinduism while keeping in mind differences even among those who sought to create a unity. The second argument was that of scholars who wanted to keep intact historicity and multiplicity of meanings within this entity called Hinduism. These two approaches were criticized by a third group of scholars who rubbished what they saw as a transcultural project of understanding non-Western religions, societies and civilizations. They felt that there was a need to create indigenous frameworks of interpretation to contest the categories created by the West. This led to a different set of problems altogether, because the question of whose interpretation would finally have primacy was left unresolved.

The most significant voice emerging out of this effort was that of Sontheimer, who argued in favour of identifying the components of Hinduism rather than being hostage to a monolithic conceptualization. Each component, he suggested, had to be seen in its own right and the dominance of a component, say a cult or a sampradaya, in a particular context minutely examined. Having made this important assertion, Sontheimer lapses into the usual romantic fantasy of Hinduism being a culture of accepted multiformity, generous liberality and tolerance between religions and ideologies.

Another conference in October 1990 at Tübingen carried forward the initiative begun in 1986.[27] It was held during the fraught period when the movement for building a Rama temple at Ayodhya was gathering momentum, and by the time the conference volume got published, the Babri Mosque had been demolished. In its pages, politics makes a conspicuous entry. Hinduism, as it seemed at that moment, was hardly tolerant and liberal. It also spoke about the sharply demarcated theological boundaries within Hinduism, where rival sects were systematically distanced, 'othering' being the technical jargon often used to refer to this process. The contributors also acknowledged a shift from what they questionably saw as a more tolerant, though elitist and hierarchically ordered Brahminic idea of co-existence to a newly valourized kshatriya ideal of self-assertion and a push for power.

Moving away from the twentieth century, one encounters the figure of Sir Monier Monier-Williams, who was born in Bombay in 1819. He studied at Calcutta, Oxford and Gottingen. He became a professor of Sanskrit, Bengali and Telugu at the East India Company's college at Haileybury, and was later the Boden Professor of Sanskrit at Oxford. He died in 1899. His *Hinduism and Its Sources*[28] is a significant attempt at naming the origins of the word 'Hindu', a step crucial to the project of presenting the picture of a unified and unitary notion of Hinduism.[29] This preoccupation at tracing the origins of the word 'Hindu' formed a crucial part of the Hindu nationalist credo and bothered all its exponents from Dayananda Saraswati to Golwalkar.

Despite the vast confluence of races, languages and social usage, asserts Monier-Williams, the Hindu religious creed remained unaffected. This was due to one language and one literature, namely Sanskrit, which preserved an original, simple, pantheistic creed. Admitting that the simplicity of

Hinduism's roots was often lost, he riled against what he saw as an 'exuberant outgrowth of monstrous mythology and a variety of polytheistic superstitions'. But the idea of a single substance, Brahman/Atman, flowing in all things, animates and inanimate, was the uncompromising creed of true Brahmanism and all orthodox Hindus (meaning, all educated Hindus) considered this as the true Veda. From the time the Vedas were first composed, Hinduism, continues Monier-Williams, had embraced something from all religions. It was all-tolerant, all-compliant, all-comprehensive and all-absorbing. Completing the circularity of the argument, what held this entity together was Sanskrit and its literature, which was the soul and mind of the Hindus. For Monier-Williams, vernacular dialects and their literature were scarcely yet deserving of the name.[30]

Addressing the Bombay branch of the Royal Asiatic Society on 25 February 1893, Paul Deussen, a professor of philosophy at the University of Keil in Germany, went several steps ahead of Monier-Williams. He argued that *Advaita Vedanta* was forever, as it was in the ancient times, living in the mind of every thoughtful Hindu. For him, all other schools of philosophy were only of historical interest. The doctrine of Adi Shankara exemplified the best and the highest in articulating *Vedanta.* He regretted that even Shankara's thought had been invaded by realistic tendencies such as *vishistadvaita*, *dvaita* and *suddhadvaita* of Ramanuja, Madhava and Vallabha; he notes with satisfaction that despite this onslaught, India had not been seduced by the misinterpreting variations of Shankara's *Advaita.*

The evidence for this overwhelming fidelity to *Advaita* comes to Deussen from a person he refers to as a well-informed, zealous adversary of Shankara's philosophy and a follower of Ramanuja. Out of every hundred Vedantins, his source tells him, fifteen follow Ramanuja, five follow Madhava, five follow Vallabha and an overwhelming seventy-five follow Shankara. So what makes the *Advaita Vedanta* of Shankara so special? Shankara's commentaries on the *Upanishads* and the *Vedanta Sutras*, elaborates Deussen, are comparable to Plato and Kant. The world is *maya*. It is unreal, the Brahman being the only reality. To know this is the way to *moksha* or liberation. This was summed up in the idea of 'Thou art that', an insight, exults Deussen, not even found in the Bible because it was tainted to a great extent by Semitic realism. Deussen translates *maya* as illusion. Plato and Kant, the best minds in occidental philosophy, had argued the same. Shankara's thought, therefore, was a wonderful coming together of Platonism and Vedantism.

Golwalkar inhabits this eighteenth- and nineteenth-century mental universe that attempted to transform Hinduism into a rigid, codified, monochromatic and aggressively masculine entity.[31] There was scarcely any room in it for diversity and plurality. Myths, legends, local colour and social variations were frowned upon, and if they were accepted selectively, they were meant to serve as tools towards forging a greater unity. The Hindu nation, therefore, had to be founded on racial and doctrinal unity, and *Advaita Vedanta* was to serve as the cementing factor in bringing this about.

Little attention was paid to the simultaneous growth of theories of inclusion and exclusion in order to reach the mythical idea of what or who constitutes a 'true' Hindu. If the systematic creation of 'out-groups' contradicted the essential elements of *Advaita*, this aberration was to be easily explained. For Swami Vivekananda, who took it upon himself to restate Hinduism, the universality of the *Brahman* rested upon recognition of Hinduism by all other faiths as the mother of all religions.[32] But for a demagogue like Golwalkar, only the eventual world imperialism of the Hindu Rashtra would make other faiths recognize the subliminal beauty of the *Advaita* philosophy.

It is important to emphasize that while notions such as 'components of Hinduism' have been introduced in discussions of Hinduism in the twentieth century, the idea of Hinduism as a tolerant, inward-looking, moksha-seeking and all-embracing faith remains largely intact. Daya Krishna, for instance, rejects the idea that Indian philosophy could be equated with a search for moksha. He affirms the development of logic from the twelfth to the seventeenth centuries as an instance of refinement of logic within Indian philosophy.[33] While there is greater awareness of inter-faith dynamics and popular manifestations of Hinduism, there is still great hesitation in even posing the question whether Hinduism, in whichever form one chooses to characterize it, does have a politics. The preponderance of this view leads to Hindutva being considered as an aberration, or even a perversion, and banishes sceptics questioning the modern formulations of Hinduism to the eternal hell of ignorance, bloody-mindedness and malafide intentions.

Correctives to this dominant view of Hinduism have always existed. In his essay titled 'Hinduism and Buddhism',[34] first delivered as a lecture in 1942, Ananda K. Coomaraswamy speaks of Hinduism as one of the oldest mystery religions and metaphysical disciplines. It has an unbroken tradition, he argues, because it is understood by millions of people, some of whom are peasants and others learned men. Having established the essentially democratic and non-dogmatic character of the faith, he begins with a series of five 'denials' about what was popularly considered to be the defining features of the faith.[35] These are:

- The Vedic doctrine is neither pantheistic nor polytheistic, nor a worship of the powers of Nature except in the sense that all powers of Nature are but the names of God's acts;
- *Karma* is not 'fate' except in the orthodox sense of the character and destiny that inhere in created things themselves, and rightly understood, determines their vocation;
- That *maya* is not illusion, but rather the material measure and means essential to the manifestation of a quantitative and, in this sense, material world of appearances comprising animate and inanimate people, creatures and objects, by which we may be either enlightened or deluded according to the degree of our own maturity;
- The notion of reincarnation in the popular sense of the return of the deceased individuals to rebirth on this earth represents only a misunderstanding of the doctrines of heredity, transmigration and regeneration;
- The six *darshanas* of the later Sanskrit 'philosophy' are not so many mutually exclusive 'systems' but, as their name implies, so many points of view which are no more mutually contradictory than are, let us say, botany and mathematics.

Kshiti Mohan Sen[36] carries the argument forward by suggesting that *bhakti* and the mystical tradition in Hinduism are as authoritative as the *dharmashastras*. In giving too much importance to texts, the religious movements of the lower strata of society had been neglected. Also, the belief in the authority of the *Upanishads* and the idea of the world as a manifestation of the *Brahman* was more a trend confined to the educated classes. This was also a direct reaction to the criticism of popular Hinduism by Christian missionaries. Sen perceived modern Hinduism to be a product of many influences, including Islam and Christianity, as also of the impact of modern science and technology, and the rise of the middle class in India.

J.L. Brockington[37] provides another significant corrective. He argues that all views attributed to Hinduism in the West are often reducible to *Advaita* because it happens to be the most familiar form of Indian thought available in the West. Contrary to popular belief, all other schools of Hindu philosophy, with the exception of *Advaita Vedanta*, were realist in outlook. Neither was the knowledge of the Vedas significant at any given point in history. Brockington shows evidence of the Hindus possessing a very perfunctory and incomplete knowledge of the Vedas from a very early date. The reference to the Vedas was imperative only in an ideal sense. This trend continued till European scholarship rediscovered the Vedas and made them central to Hindu thought, something that the Hindu nationalist accepted unconditionally. But before this happened, most earlier and later schools of Hindu philosophy rejected the authority of the Vedas. In fact, the Vedas were invoked primarily to give respectability to later innovations; their inaccessibility and inadequate knowledge facilitated an almost endless reinterpretation of doctrine.

Golwalkar's Hinduism was not a living entity. It depended on the idea of a Hindu Golden Age, from which every subsequent development was seen as an onward march of degeneration and decadence. His project was to recapture this imaginary past. Ironically, however, even his conception of the past was one that was created by European Indologists. The Indologists were usually classicists, who saw nothing of merit in contemporary India and hankered after a past that had been lost due to a rupture with what they considered as the 'classical' past. Most Indologists were also men of religion and strove to bring Hinduism in line with the Biblical tradition and Mosaic history. They did not baulk at distorting 'Hindu' chronology to accommodate and bring Hinduism into the fold of Old Testament dating. For instance, all Asiatic people were said to have descended from Shem, one of the three sons of Noah. The positing of a Hindu Golden Age was thus used as a way to find justification for a Hinduism which was monotheistic, equalitarian and non-idolatrous.[38] Any subsequent development was considered as a deviation from the grand ideals of the past. The Hinduism that emerged as a result of the criticism by Christian missionaries and the efforts of the Indologists had a greater resemblance to the model of Semitic religions. Apologists of a certain brand of Hindu nationalism, like Golwalkar, never cared to question or acknowledge this distortion. While there is much in Golwalkar that vampires on Hindu texts, images and terms, it hardly ever approximates to a full understanding of the evolution of tradition and its breaks and departures. In the end, understanding was subordinated to the imperatives of nationalism.

If Golwalkar's understanding of Hinduism was derivative of the way in which European philosophers and Indologists portrayed the 'religion of the Hindus', then his sense of the nation was also entirely borrowed from a certain strand of romantic nationalism articulated in Europe during the eighteenth and nineteenth centuries. This also holds true for his vision of the Hindu Rashtra, which was circumscribed by the idea of the dissolution of individuality in society and nation, the primacy of the nation and its worship, belief in ideas of purity, sincerity, integrity, martyrdom, and the drive forward to sacrifice everything for the sake of an ideal. Despite resorting to selectively chosen quotes from texts as varied as the *Rig Veda*, the *Mahabharata*, the *Ramayana* and the *Vishnupurana* to argue in favour of the antiquity of the Hindu Rashtra, Golwalkar's project is, in reality, an attempt to approximate to a modern idea of the nation wrapped in antiquarian clothes.

To understand Golwalkar's debt to theories of romantic nationalism so fashionable during his time, it would be useful to briefly digress in order to consider the ideas of some of the seminal philosophers who spawned theories of romantic nationalism. The central figure in this was the German philosopher and historian, Johann Gottfried von Herder[39] (1744–1803). He perceived the human ability to express oneself fully as a fundamental function of being human. Any restrictions on the capacity to express oneself were an undesirable constraint. The question of expressing oneself went hand in hand with where one belonged. Songs, dances, morals, symbols and institutions were made consciously or unconsciously by individuals or groups. It was often difficult to attribute authorship to certain elements within a group or among a people. If answers were to be found for their origin, these would, inevitably, lie in the realm of nameless antiquity. Nevertheless, the world is made the way people have intended it to be. More specifically, the German or the Russian or the Indian world was made by Germans, Russians and Indians and exhibited certain features that were specific to their context.

Herder suggested that every human being seeks to belong to a larger entity, be it a group, nation, movement or sect. It was within the nature of humans to belong, to identify for themselves natural roots, and have a sense of being 'at home'. His conception of the 'nation' is not based on the criterion of blood or race, but on the common bonds of language and land. But the implication of this view was that those who belonged to a particular cluster of people were more responsible for their existence than those who shared little with this specific *gestalt* or organized whole. This view suggested that differences rather than similarities help humans in understanding people who are very dissimilar to themselves.

Immanuel Kant (1724–1804) was Herder's contemporary at the University of Königsberg. He argued that human beings are human only because of their capacity for choice. Only humans choose what they wish to choose, and it is this act of choice that distinguishes them from all other objects in nature. It is will that enables humans to choose between good and evil, and morality is a direct outcome of this choice. Therefore, humans ought to determine their own lives and be responsible for their own acts. Values are similarly created through the act of humans choosing. The highest manifestation of this free exercise of choice is self-determination.

These two thinkers had a profound influence on the subsequent unfolding of nationalism and the consciousness of nationhood in a 'pathological state of inflammation'.[40] Friedrich Schiller (1775–1854) carried forward Kant's idea of the individual's moral autonomy to his notion of spiritual freedom. Humans must resist all that oppresses them. This is moral defiance, where an individual or a group defies in the name of an exalted ideal to which there is unflinching commitment and, if need be, lays down one's life for the ideal. The notions of heroism and martyrdom as desirable and admirable ends emerge under the influence of this view.

For Johann Gottleib Fichte (1762–1814), perfect individual freedom was an impossibility because nature had manifold ways of restraining and confining humans. The individual became aware of himself only when something that was not the self tried to create an obstacle in the path of the individual. This resistance could come in the way of realizing oneself or in the individual's effort to dominate, conquer or mould an object or a person. It is this clash that creates a sense of the self and the not-self. Perfect freedom, however, is elusive and can only be attained through identifying oneself with something that is larger and greater than the mere individual. He calls it 'spirit'. But spirit for him was not the spirit of an individual because the personalized spirit was full of imperfections and was imprisoned within a body. Rather, the spirit was something that a collectivity commonly shared. An individual, then, is a mere speck of sand in a vast desert. Therefore, customs, traditions, habits and all other elements that constitute an individual are also the creation of many other individuals. In identifying with a larger spirit, the individual forms an organic unity with that collectivity. In other words, the individual, for Fichte, could be spoken of only in terms of entities such as a nation, a sect or a class.

Freedom was not just contemplating the idea of an autonomous individual. Fichte argued that freedom was to act, to create and leave the impress of one's will upon the world. But the individual had to cease being an empirical entity and become part of a larger whole like the nation. Once this leap was taken, it was the nation or class or sect that acted. It was no longer individual freedom that was at stake but the freedom of the nation. Just as individuals constantly faced obstruction and resistance, and facing these challenges created a sense of the self, so, too, did nations. In order to assert themselves and move forward, nations had to wage war in order to impose their will and personality upon the world. Those who managed to assert themselves and fight the barriers created by recalcitrant reality were the *urvolk* or the primal people; they were free and capable of action. The others were a mere 'annexe to life'[41] and were strangers and outsiders. It takes but one step from here to reach the twentieth-century fascist idea of an 'in-group' and an 'out-group', defined famously by the jurist and philosopher Carl Schmitt as the relation between 'friend' and 'foe'.

Golwalkar's ideal of the Hindu Rashtra drew sustenance from this dark and fraught set of ideas.[42] These were channeled and disseminated through theories of cultural nationalism current in the nineteenth and twentieth centuries in India. But their seeds could be traced to several strands of Enlightenment thought, the French Revolution, and to the dominant themes of romanticism. These ideas percolated in India through the more obvious examples of European men of action such as Napoleon, Garibaldi and Mazzini, and through the attempts of men like Sri Aurobindo, Swami Vivekananda and V.D. Savarkar to articulate an idea of the nation during the colonial period.[43]

In the maturing and development of Golwalkar's vision of the Hindu Rashtra, figures like Swami Vivekananda, Sri Aurobindo, Bal Gangadhar Tilak, Madan Mohan Malaviya and Savarkar played an important role. These thinkers had already formulated an ideal of the nation on the basis of Hindu foundations. Golwalkar saw in their thought a set of common features and defining characteristics for his conception of the Hindu Rashtra. For him, Swami Vivekananda was the clearest and most forceful exponent of the idea of worship of the Motherland as God and as *punyabhoomi* or holy land[44]. In Vivekananda, he perceived the first clear articulation of the rejection of mental slavery to foreign ideas and what he called *abharatiya* tendencies.

Vivekananda also figures in Golwalkar's thought as the inspiration for his support of the caste system, the accent on physical strength, the first clear enunciation of the Hindu

Rashtra ideal and *seva* or service as a way of consolidating Hindu society around religion and culture. Most of all, he perceives in Vivekananda the vision of delineating a unique destiny for the nation based on a clear understanding of the history and way of life enshrined in the timeless tenets of Hindu thought and action. Similarly, Sri Aurobindo's thought represented for Golwalkar a perfect antidote for cultural amnesia and modern forms of secularism. In Golwalkar's reading of Aurobindo, the Maharishi was seen as an unambiguous votary of the ancient sanatana dharma as the basis of national life in this country.

Tilak also appears crucially in Golwalkar's pantheon of Hindu nationalist icons. He gives Tilak the same status as Kumarila Bhatt, Adi Shankaracharya and Shivaji, who, like his illustrious predecessors, removed *rashtravismarana* or national amnesia and *atmavismriti* or amnesia about the self. Tilak was not the only one to speak of *swarajya* or self-rule, says Golwalkar, but he was unique in privileging an unadulterated ideal of Hindu Rashtra based on national *sanskriti*, *parampara* and *dharma*. Madan Mohan Malaviya also exemplified the same ideal and had the audacity, exults Golwalkar, to name his university 'Banaras Hindu University', where 'Hindu' had no connotation other than 'nation' and 'national'.

Finally, Golwalkar acknowledges Savarkar's unique contribution in systematically formulating the ideal of the Hindu Rashtra, and more importantly, for arguing in favour of adopting a militant Hindu nationalist stand. As early as 1929, there is evidence of Golwalkar regularly corresponding with Savarkar in connection with the latter's writings.[45] Writing elsewhere in 1970, he recognized in Savarkar the finest contemporary articulation and vision of the real identity of the nation.[46] But even before joining the Sangh and prior to the emergence of national socialism and fascism as decisive historical forces, Golwalkar was exhorting his friends like Baburao Telang in a manner reminiscent of Savarkar: 'Friends, raise the nation, make money, gather strength, organise, remove enmity among castes. Serve Motherland and Hindu Dharma.'[47]

Critics have often seen striking resemblances in Golwalkar's thought with fascism. Christophe Jaffrelot in his excellent study of Hindu nationalism and Indian politics[48] seeks to trace the German sources of Golwalkar's ideology. This is based almost entirely on a reading, and correctly so, of *We or Our Nationhood Defined* as a text attributed to Golwalkar. Even if this particular text was to be removed from the Golwalkar oeuvre, his idea of endless sacrifice of individuality in the service and love of the nation, his argument about the intrinsic superiority of Hindus over all other people, the tone of millenarian fanaticism and religious frenzy that mark all his formulations, the obsessive accent on youth and the constant harping on conspiracies against the Hindu nation are themes that share a distinct resonance with fascism. Golwalkar often dismissed these charges as name-calling and abuse, though he betrayed a sneaking admiration for much of the central ideas of fascism.

This charge, however, distracts from the derivative nature of Golwalkar's enterprise. For example, even the idea of the state as a mystical institution was evident in the thought of such theorists as Adam Müller, who was a German disciple of Edmund Burke. To reduce the nation state to a set of laws or to a written constitution, argued Müller, was an attempt doomed to failure. The only constitution of any consequence, he continued, was the one that resided in the hearts of human beings living together as a passionate mystical family. In other words, there is nothing uniquely fascist about these ideas.

Rather, they are part of the same continuum that surfaced in the eighteenth century and culminated in the hysterical self-assertion and nihilism of Hitler and Mussolini in the twentieth century. Golwalkar and the Sangh remain the residual standard-bearers of this destructive impulse.

Once this model of nationalism was accepted, every symptom of romantic excess crept into Golwalkar's ideas. His emphasis on integrity, sincerity, sacrifice and authenticity are merely obvious manifestations of the malady. The lack of interest in political power, rejection of any legitimate democratic authority, purity of soul as the only arbiter of all things, unity without legality and undiluted idealism are the other malignant signs of the same disease. Like the great figures of German romanticism, Golwalkar constantly saw his life's mission and that of the Sangh as an interminable fight between the forces of light and darkness. Politics was replaced by the vision of a religious crusade, where only collective salvation was possible. Only Golwalkar and the Sangh were 'true', 'real' and 'pure', and only they knew where the good of the nation lay. The Indian nation might have been created in 1947, but for Golwalkar, Hindus were not sovereigns in that nation. His task was to 'liberate' Hindu society and establish the Hindu Rashtra. He saw this as his divinely ordained mission and dedicated his life to chasing a chimera that was his own creation.

When he died in 1973, Golwalkar left behind a Sangh that was bereft of an ideologue of his stature. Despite this intellectual vacuum, the Sangh continued to present a picture of ideological clarity and certitude. A closer look, however, reveals a greater degree of ambiguity within the Sangh over questions of ideology and politics than appearances suggest.

At the level of ideology, there was a clear split between those who styled themselves nationalists or rashtravaadis and those who professed their allegiance to Hindutva. The nationalists claimed that the term 'Hindu' merely constitutes the cultural matrix and identity marker for India. They referred to the Sangh founder's insistence that 'Hindu' refers to an unbroken civilizational heritage of India that binds people emotionally with a common history and a shared civilizational identity.

The Hindutva votaries claimed that while the Sangh rejected Savarkar's idea of *punyabhoomi* or holy land, a concept that automatically excludes Muslims and Christians from being part of the putative Hindu Rashtra, it would be a great error to abdicate the claims of Hindus as the 'original' founders of this nation in favour of any abstract and formal notion of nationalism. This was the conclusion Golwalkar arrived at in the seven-day conclave of the Sangh at Thane in October 1972.

Semantics apart, there seemed little difference between the two views other than a question of emphasis. Nothing, however, explains the subtle difference between the two views better than former BJP President L.K. Advani's formulation that while Hindutva for him represented idealism, nationalism was his ideology. Advani's typology illustrated the schism, not merely within the BJP, but also within the Sangh. A senior Sangh member and historian of the Sangh, Dilip Deodhar, likens this to grafting an apple tree on to a mango tree[49].

After Hedgewar's death in 1940, this subtle distinction has constantly been in play within the RSS, with an unspoken 'war' being constantly waged for dominance of one over the other. Golwalkar's stature, however, managed to paper over differences and keep the lid firmly shut on any major ideological and organizational conflagration. This seeming sense of ideological unity and organizational idyll, however, has led to many misconceptions, chiefly that the Sangh functions on the basis of ideology and its practices are governed by a strict fidelity to its core principles. This is not to suggest that the Sangh does not harbour a telos, an ultimate goal or purpose; that is articulated as the vision of making India a great power.

In its day-to-day functioning, the Sangh embodies the notion of transience, or *mayavaad.* Following this, there is nothing that it swears eternal allegiance to, except the supremacy of the organization. In this sense, whatever the organization says becomes ideology. It takes its cue from Chhatrapati Shivaji's strategy of 'hit and run'. Absolute commitment to any issue or principle is seen, therefore, to be detrimental to the goal of making India a great power. In recent years, this has become the commonly accepted view in the Sangh's interface with politics as well.

A dominant view among sections of the Sangh as well as independent commentators is that Golwalkar's departure in 1973 marked the advent of ideological dilution and rise of pragmatism in the Sangh. Balasaheb Deoras, Rajju Bhaiyya and K.S. Sudarshan are seen as distinct from the 'saintly' and 'cerebral' Golwalkar, and therefore, less committed to the word and spirit of the original canon delineated by Hedgewar and Golwalkar. This is far from true. The first rupture with ideology came as early as 1948. The event that triggered this subtle paradigm shift was the murder of Mahatma Gandhi by Nathuram Godse, and the subsequent ban on the Sangh for nearly a year. During the course of this year, Golwalkar spent time in prison.[50]

After his release in July 1949, Golwalkar gave a series of lectures in Nagpur in October 1949. He observed that Gandhi's murder and the subsequent ban on the Sangh had shaken the Sangh and made it jittery and weak. Twenty years of relentless work had been compromised by a 'small crisis'.[51] This had led to doubts in the minds of Sangh followers and workers about the relevance and efficacy of the 'work' itself. Golwalkar terms this as a lack of confidence and self-belief. To overcome this, he suggests a way out. Apart from the usual exhortation to eschew selfishness, individual opinions and lack of unity, he also advocates gentle and affectionate persuasion in order to bring about organizational unity and cohesion. But this was not enough. Golwalkar clearly asks the Sangh members to 'abandon their rigidity of views'[52] and desist from being stubborn. I am neither an optimist nor a pessimist, but a realist, he declared.

Speaking in Uttar Pradesh between 23 December 1949 and 2 January 1950, Golwalkar admitted that before the ban on the Sangh in 1948, Sangh workers had become indifferent to the external environment as also to the internal contradictions within the organization. He regretted that the very people, namely, the Hindus, for whom the Sangh worked tirelessly, had not strenuously opposed the ban, and some of them had even actively worked to destroy the Sangh. The answer to this lay in the lack of values, morals and character in the fragmented Hindu society. The ban on the Sangh, he argued, was a result of disinformation and distortion and it provided an opportunity for the *abharatiya*, afraid of the growth and reach of the Sangh, to destroy it.

In a reference to Godse, he says that the Sangh had nothing to do with 'the man who killed the Mahatma'.[53] He was the office-bearer of another organization, argues Golwalkar, and yet nothing happened to that organization. The allusion here is to the Hindu Mahasabha. The ban on the Sangh, he concludes, was indicative of the power of the Sangh's work and was deliberate and an excuse to contain the Sangh. In an interview given much later,[54] Golwalkar reiterated that Godse had been a member of the Sangh ten years before he murdered the Mahatma. Being a non-political person, he saw no opposition between himself and Gandhi. Having said this, Golwalkar went a step further. He declared that he considered Gandhiji a great man and that 'I have respect for him in my heart'.[55]

Several years after Nathuram Godse's hanging for the murder of Gandhi, his brother, Gopal Godse, claimed that his brother had really never left the Sangh and that his statements suggesting the contrary were a way of easing pressure on the Sangh, which had been banned following the Mahatma's murder.[56] Indeed, when Nathuram Godse walked to the gallows, he did so singing the Sangh song, '*Namaste sadaavatsalematrubhoome* (I bow to you always, O loving Motherland).'

It is true that there was profound distrust between the Sangh and the Hindu Mahasabha after Golwalkar took over the Sangh's leadership.[57] The Hindu Mahasabha leadership did not share the same rapport with Golwalkar as they did with Hedgewar. Despite this, Nathuram Godse made tireless efforts to bring the two organizations together.[58] In 1938, he wrote to Savarkar to assume the leadership of the Hindus, including an alignment with the Sangh, in order to realize the goal of establishing a Hindu Rashtra. In a letter written on 10 July 1938, Godse pleads with Savarkar for a more militant stand on the part of the Hindu nationalists, something that would attract younger people to the Hindu nationalist fold. 'The only organization in Maharashtra as well as in all Hindustan that is capable of uniting the Hindus', says the future killer of the Mahatma, 'is the Rashtriya Swayamsevak Sangh'.[59] In characteristically dramatic fashion, he tells Savarkar that only Dr. Hedgewar was his equal. If only Savarkar could speak to

Hedgewar and bring about Hindu unity, a lot could be achieved towards realizing the goal of a Hindu Rashtra.

The more militant sections among the Hindu nationalists have continued to valourize Godse. Bal Thackeray declared in 1992 that future generations would install Godse's statues rather than of Gandhi. The Nathuram Godse Memorial meeting held on 17 November 1993, which saw laudatory speeches for Godse, produced a sharp reaction from the then BJP president, L.K. Advani: 'Nathuram Godse was a bitter critic of the Rashtriya Swayamsevak Sangh. ... His charge was that the RSS had made Hindus impotent. We have had nothing to do with Godse.'[60]

Koenraad Elst, an unabashed apologist of Godse, quotes Craig Baxter's view that Gandhi's murder has been a millstone around the neck of the Hindu nationalists, and more so of the RSS.[61] Elst is of the view that Godse never rejected the Sangh, and while he may not formally have been part of the organization in the years leading to Gandhi's murder, ideologically he remained an RSS man unto the last.[62] Elst goes even further, castigating the Sangh for being apologetic about Godse and for being defensive about the charge of complicity in the Mahatma's murder:

> The RSS family's line has been just the opposite [as contrasted with the line taken by Bal Thackeray]: they have exhausted themselves in denials and condemnations of the murder. Because of their enemies' persistence, this has meant that in this respect, as in many others, the RSS family has been continually on the defensive. In fact, seeing the RSS on the defensive has obviously fuelled their opponents' gusto in using this allegation. ... To prove its innocence, the RSS family has invested a lot of words denouncing the murder and praising the Mahatma. ... Years later he [Golwalkar] still gave speeches

> in praise of the Mahatma, just like any average Congressman. In his case, however, no outsider was willing to credit him with sincerity, perhaps wrongly.[63]

Praise of Gandhi notwithstanding, everything Golwalkar formulated in his quest to attain the utopian Hindu Rashtra stood in sharp contrast to Gandhi's thought and action. In a recent article[64], the historian Ramachandra Guha has cited a police report that points to a meeting of the Sangh which Golwalkar addressed in the town of Govardhan on 6 December 1947, where he discussed ways to 'assassinate the leading persons of the Congress in order to terrorise the public and to get their hold over them.' Neither was the Sangh a mere cultural organization before and after the Partition. Andersen and Damle have pointed out the manner in which Sangh members in Sindh manufactured bombs, collected weapons and made hand grenades.[65] More recently, Rita Kothari, writing on the RSS in Sindh between 1942 and 1948, notes the irony of the Sangh members 'moving from a simple drill to manufacturing ammunition, of moving from devices of defence to those of attack...'[66] Golwalkar on his part continued to deny any role in pre-Partition riots, but also continued to justify violence as a way of bringing about change:

> In an emergency, to remove a social malaise, violence in the form of surgery may be essential. But it has to be controlled violence. One who takes recourse to violence must know the quantity and extent to which it is used and when to stop it.[67]

Golwalkar's first substantive comment is to be found in a letter written to Baburao Telang on 16 March 1929. He writes about the many mistakes Gandhi may have made in politics but says that 'there can be no doubt about his authenticity'. It is on the basis of this authenticity, he continues, that Gandhiji feels he can obtain independence through ahimsa, non-cooperation and the charkha; that is the reason he says all these things and does not care if people laugh at him.[68] Between then and 30 January 1948, there is very little evidence of any real admiration for Gandhi on Golwalkar's part, except for calling him 'vishwavandaniya' or one who is praised across the world, during an address to the Sangh Shiksha Varg in 1946.

Golwalkar was in Madras attending a tea party in his honour at the Ramakrishna Lunch Home when the news of Gandhi's assassination came. He sent a telegram to Nehru, Sardar Patel and Devdas Gandhi, the Mahatma's son, in which he expressed shock and sorrow at the 'cruel fatal attack on a great personality'.[69] He directed all Sangh branches to suspend all daily activities for thirteen days in order to express sorrow at the 'sad death of revered Mahatmaji'.[70] He wrote a letter the next day from Nagpur to Nehru.[71] He calls the killer of the Mahatma an 'unthinking corrupt-hearted individual'. The act was beyond forgiveness and was hateful. If this black act had been committed, he argues, by someone from an enemy nation, even then it would not be condonable. The Mahatma's life, he continues, was not confined to a particular community but transcended these limits to the service of all humanity. Golwalkar saw the attack on Gandhi not just as an attack on an individual but as an act of treachery against the entire nation. He goes one step further. He exhorts Nehru to deal with the Mahatma's murderer in an appropriate fashion. 'However hard the treatment meted out to him may be', writes Golwalkar, 'it would seem mild in comparison to the loss suffered'.[72]

In similar vein, he wrote to Sardar Patel as well, calling the Mahatma's murder an evil act, which he was at a loss of words to condemn. In a statement to the Associated Press on 1 February 1948, Golwalkar regretted that the 'villain [of the act of murdering the Mahatma] is not merely a citizen of this country, but also a Hindu. He called Godse an individual with a deformed state of mind.

Golwalkar's categorical comments on Godse and his public repudiation of Godse's act seem to confirm Elst's contentious view that Golwalkar took to praising the Mahatma after his murder and that the opponents of the Sangh have unjustly doubted his sincerity. In this context, it would be instructive to look at a speech Golwalkar gave on 6 October 1969 at Sangli to commemorate the Gandhi centenary. In the same month he also wrote an essay in *Yugavani*, published from Nagpur.

In the speech at Sangli,[73] Golwalkar calls Gandhi '*praatahsmaraniya*' or worthy of being invoked in the morning. He argues that just as pure thoughts and great people are invoked as part of tradition in the morning, so should Gandhi be invoked as part of this morning ritual. The Sangh, he informs his audience, had gone ahead and included the Mahatma's name as part of their 'Bharat Bhakti Stotra' or the hymn for worship of the Motherland. The Mahatma, he continues, turned dust into gold and was worthy of being included in the pantheon of the great.

But he was great, argues Golwalkar, because of his rootedness within the Hindu faith. The Mahatma's nationalism was but a natural extension of his faith. His love of humanity also flowed from his being a staunch Hindu. In fact, the Mahatma had predicted that Hinduism might seem enfeebled today but would emerge glorious one day. To fulfill the Mahatma's dream of the greater glory of Hinduism was the mission of the Sangh, he concludes.

The essay in *Yugavani*[74] is easily comparable to Godse's statement in court during his trial[75]. It follows the same structure as Godse's statement, where overt praise for the greatness of the Mahatma camouflages a severe indictment. It begins by calling the Mahatma one of the great souls to be born in the last fifty to seventy-five years in India. He acknowledges the impact Gandhi had on the ordinary life and politics of the country; he was a man of many parts and a multifaceted personality.

Having eulogized the Mahatma at the outset, Golwalkar proceeds to argue that even those who were singularly dedicated to him and worshipped him had started to despair and to get weary of his views. This included Madam Mohan Malaviya, Nehru and Sardar Patel. Gandhi's insistence on giving Rs 55 crore to Pakistan had caused Patel great agony. This Golwalkar claims from firsthand knowledge of the Sardar's mind on the issue. But Gandhi did not commit an error only at the time of Partition, he says, and begins to list out the Mahatma's errors from the very beginning.

His first great mistake was to support the British during World War I. He ought to have taken advantage of the enemy's weakness and asked for independence. Tilak had opposed Gandhi on this question. Non-cooperation too was a great error. It had inculcated in students and other sections of society a fondness for indiscipline, lack of character and anarchy, a Gandhian legacy that led to the destruction of the life of citizens in the country after independence. Similarly, Gandhi was a staunch Hindu and respected all faiths. This is why he chose to forget the history of a thousand years and decided to draw Muslims into the national fold. The consequence of this was the Partition and subsequent moves on the part of politicians to appease minorities.

The essay ends with a mixture of praise and indictment. He was right in arguing for the protection of cows, correct in his campaign for removing untouchability and praiseworthy in giving voice to the weak. But his impracticality, ironically, stemmed from his self-confidence, his rootedness in the Hindu faith and his ready public admission of his mistakes.

This realism, in short, is Golwalkar's legacy to the Sangh as well as the Hindu nationalists. Following this, the Sangh, as well as the Sangh Parivar, devised a formula that prevents any absolute commitment to a single ideological position. When in power, the Sangh Parivar swore allegiance to nationalism, and while out of power it propagated Hindutva. This was partly to do with the constraints of coalition politics that had emerged in recent years but also circumscribed by incommensurable views on what constitutes orthodoxy for the Sangh Parivar.

The only ideology that the Sangh truly follows is *sanghvaad* or the primacy of the organization. This is best illustrated by the Sangh's response to the question of dual membership (Jan Sangh members were also *swayamsevaks*) raised during the Janata Party regime in 1977, of which the Jan Sangh was a part. A remarkable pamphlet written by Baburao Chauthaiwale (*Maine dekhe huye param pujaniya Shri Balasaheb Deoras*), a close associate and aide of the then Sangh chief, Balasaheb Deoras, delineates the flexibility of the Sangh in dealing with questions of ideology and the Sangh's pragmatism. In response to the controversy over dual membership, the Sangh took the following decisions:

- Other than what was deemed absolutely necessary, swayamsevaks within the Sangh ought not to associate with the Sangh in any special way;
- Senior Sangh officials will only refer to Hindutva's essence in public lectures and fora perfunctorily and only in passing and concentrate more on questions of organization.

There was resentment in the Sangh on the question of abandoning Hindutva as well as other core values, though this arrangement continued only for one and a half years. The chief of the Maharashtra wing of the Sangh, Kaka Limaye, wrote to Deoras protesting this move and asking him to fashion another organization, telling him in no uncertain terms to 'leave Doctorji's [Sangh founder, Dr. Hedgewar] sangh for the Hindus to us'. Baburao Chauthaiwale exults over the fact that Sangh leaders, normally considered apolitical and inept in political matters, had out maneuvered politically astute leaders like Madhu Limaye and Raj Narayan.

This brings us to the second rupture. Invoking Lord Krishna's explanation of his relationship to existence as explained in the Bhagavad Gita, Golwalkar had seen the interface between the Sangh and Sangh-inspired organizations like the Jan Sangh thus: 'I am in all that exists and they are in me, but I am not in them and they are not in me.' He perceived such affiliates as 'additions' and not substitutes to the mission and goals of the Sangh: a lofty distance existed between the Sangh and organizations claiming allegiance to it. While he argued that the Sangh needed power in order to influence every aspect of society, he also dreamt of a future when the government of the day would take orders from the Sangh. Only this would lead to the achievement of the Sangh's goal—uniting Hindus into a Hindu Rashtra.

That goal might still lurk in the background, but the Sangh of present *sarsanghchalak* Mohan Bhagwat and the BJP of Narendra Modi have effectively erased the distance between the principal and its affiliate: now, the Sangh is the BJP and the BJP is the Sangh. In doing so, Golwalkar's idea of fashioning the Sangh on an ideal of renunciation and asceticism has been finally buried. Purity, virtue, inculcation of values, cultural awakening–these have become mere words with occasional rhetorical currency but little substance. Golwalkar had likened politics to a woman of questionable character, one who takes on various guises to entice and please. The Sangh no longer has a problem with such questionable cohabitation.

Further, Golwalkar believed the Sangh had the divine mission of wielding *dharmadand* or righteous control over politics and society, even if it was to be indirect. He saw lack of control as a consequence of diversity and democracy, which had wrecked Hindu unity and introduced un-Hindu ideas and forces. Bhagwat and Modi have dispensed with this article of faith as well. Righteous control has been replaced with unscrupulous pragmatism and political ambition: the *dand* remains; the *dharma* lies subservient to *dand*.

To understand the Modi–Sangh axis is to understand the radical transformation that has swept the Sangh. The Sangh now perceives Golwalkar as an aberration. It has completed the change from a moralizing, sanctimonious and self-righteous outfit to a ruthless political outfit that acknowledges the pragmatism of Golwalkar's successor as *sarsanghchalak*, Balasaheb Deoras: the Sangh had to be free of idealism, ideology and scruples to achieve its Hindu Rashtra. The Modi–Bhagwat combine has advanced this further by outsourcing fragments of the original ideology to anyone who wishes to implement it. Modi, then, can selectively speak of both robust nationalism and of development. Former Madhya Pradesh Chief Minister Shivraj Singh Chouhan felt free to ride the development plank while introducing the singing of Vande Mataram in schools. B.S. Yeddyurappa is allowed to mine minerals and simultaneously change textbooks to suit a Hindutva orientation. Under Modi, with the Sangh openly calling the shots, what emerges is piecemeal Hindutva. This is how it works: the Sangh and the BJP have modified their conception of politics and their already apologetic idea of democracy to one preferred by corporate India. Development and progress are then only thinly veiled euphemisms for technocratic-managerial governance and pursuit of unbridled self-interest. The rhetoric of a strong India as a future superpower legitimizes the development agenda. In orchestrating this subletting of politics to corporate India, the Sangh–BJP propaganda machine has skilfully transformed politics and the politician into the enemy while painting themselves as guardians of a future India that increasingly resembles a corporate boardroom.

Finally, there's the attempt to portray Modi in the flattering tones of a righteous kshatriya ruler, forever at war with the internal and external enemies of the nation. Sardar Patel and Indira Gandhi might be the inspirations for firmness and decisiveness, but the overall picture is of a kshatriya king battling to save his kingdom from mostly imagined enemies. This is a consequence of the rejection of the asceticism represented by Golwalkar, who for a brief period was a sanyasi influenced by Swami Vivekananda's philosophy. In contrast, Modi's spin doctors present him as brave, unsparing, accurate, virile, righteous and fearsome.

Here lies the ultimate triumph of Savarkar's mode of Hindutva. It is one that accords primacy to politics, adversarial nationalism, Western technological modernity and violence as legitimate ways of envisioning and realizing a Hindu Rashtra. This leaves the question of Golwalkar's legacy open. Was he the idealist he is made out to be, or was he a realist as he himself claimed? Has the Sangh finally capitulated to Savarkar's extreme political nationalism or will it continue to rhetorically swear by a diluted version of Golwalkar's realism masquerading as cultural Hindu nationalism? Given the Sangh's schizophrenia, it is safe to say that Golwalkar's thought will continue to serve as the Sangh's ideal, resurrected conveniently for rhetorical purposes. Savarkar, in turn, will serve as the ideological and political mentor of the Sangh. Golwalkar and Savarkar stand side by side, their irreconcilable differences in life effortlessly resolved, many years after their death, by the politics of our times.

1

When Salt Dissolves in Water

Golwalkar wrote a set of three letters addressed to the Sangh on 2 April 1973. These letters were to be read only after he had passed on. Death came three months later, on 6 June 1973, and these letters, which constituted his will and testament, were opened.

While all the three letters deal with matters relating to the Sangh and its future functioning, a passage in the second letter stands out. It reiterates an abiding article of Golwalkar's faith and worldview, namely, the dissolution of the individual in a larger whole. He exhorts the Sangh only to worship the nation and pursue the goal of creating a unified Hindu society. There is no place in the organization for piety to be directed towards an individual. Hence, the Sangh is to desist from building a memorial for him.

Self

In the years leading up to his death, Golwalkar constantly harped on the theme of the supremacy of society over the individual. No human being is eternal, he told the Sangh Shiksha Varg in 1971, and only the life-flow of society is eternal. An individual must inevitably die, what remains is the unity of a society expressed in its collectivity. In 1972, he quotes an English saying suggesting that life is to be seen as an accident and death as the rule. The individual is an organism prone to weakness and death, but only a unified society and nation can conquer the weakness by which individuals are inevitably assailed.

The metaphor of dissolution of individuality in favour of a collectivity, be it an organization or society or nation, is the foundation on which Golwalkar was to construct his ideal of the Hindu Rashtra. Addressing the Sangh in 1954, he likened the annihilation of individuality in favour of the nation to a piece of salt falling in water and losing its existence. What remains of the salt is just the taste, he noted, but the physical form withers away completely.

There were people who considered loss of individuality as good as being dead. Golwalkar thought of this as a mistaken notion. Thirty-five years before writing his last will and testament, he addressed the Sangh on 10 June 1938, in the presence of its founder, Dr K.B. Hedgewar. In the clearest exposition of his idea of the supremacy of the collectivity, he argued that dissolution of individuality was the true indicator of a nation's welfare and progress. In doing so, one ceases to remain an individual; the individual becomes the nation itself.

This was the ideal Swami Akhandananda had presented to Golwalkar during his stay at Sargachhi in 1936–37. Once while Golwalkar was taking the Lord's name, Akhandananda asked him to forget God and rinse the vessels first. When Golwalkar had done that, the Swami asked him to sweep, clean and water the garden. When Golwalkar had done all these tasks without showing the slightest disinterest or disinclination, Akhandananda asked him to remember God. Golwalkar narrates this incident and suggests that nothing ought to be kept for oneself—neither heart nor body nor even mind. Everything ought to be handed over to the collectivity of which one is a part. An individual ought to be like a stone which can be placed anywhere without its offering the slightest resistance.

For Golwalkar, the sublimation of the 'I' and 'mine' was the highest goal of every Hindu. Giving up individuality was the ultimate spiritual destination towards which every Hindu ought to ceaselessly and tirelessly work. True life lay in *tyaag* or sacrifice. The notions of 'I' and 'mine' were mired in the sensuous and material world. The world of the senses puts limits on us, he observes, and prevents us from taking the inevitable leap. To be a slave of the 'I' and 'mine' is equivalent to being a slave of nature. Excellence lies in control over nature; one who rises high must go against nature, exhibit true manliness and justify one's human birth. Authenticity and transcendence lies in sublimating the 'I' and 'mine' in favour of society and nation. This does not necessarily mean that the 'I' gets completely eliminated. In fact, it gets enlarged in the form of the nation and society. The movement, then, is from individual to society to world spirit or divinity.

Golwalkar illustrates the idea of unity and oneness through an example from the time of Ramakrishna Paramahansa. A sadhu once came to the Kali temple. He used to read a voluminous text every day. All philosophy and metaphysics seemed contained in this tome. But the sadhu never allowed anyone to touch this text. Some young men stealthily sought to find out what the text contained. When they managed to get hold of the mysterious book, they discovered that only 'OM' was written on all its pages. They asked the holy man why there was no philosophical or metaphysical matter written in the text. The sadhu told them that all he needed to read was the symbol 'OM'. That alone removed all his doubts and his ignorance. He experienced a sense of completeness in *Omkar.* All other writing was mere word play.

In his relentless rejection of individuality,[1] uniqueness, originality and whimsicality in favour of the stampede of oneness, collectivity and unity, Golwalkar also betrays a deep distrust of diversity. As long as there is diversity and plurality, he argues, true character cannot be formed, for these propensities breed selfishness, which is the greatest impediment to a radical and unequivocal love of the nation. For true nationalism to arise, all society ought to be considered one and everyone should be seen as the same.

The word that Golwalkar uses to indicate diversity is *bhinnataa,* which could be variously translated to mean separateness, difference, distinction or dissimilarity. However, seen in the context of the totality of his thought, diversity is the correct translation. Given his rejection of democracy, and his typology of modernity as permissiveness, his views of individualism and diversity are essential ingredients for his vision of radical unity.

Society

Golwalkar was clear that the Hindu Rashtra had existed since time immemorial and was the repository of lofty ideals. It was exemplified by an unbroken tradition. Despite the existence of a continuous tradition, the Hindu Rashtra of his imagination had been enslaved due to foreign invasions and the loss of cultural memory. This had to be explained, not merely to make sense of the past, but also in order to recapture the ideal of the Hindu Rashtra and restore it to its pre-Islamic and pre-colonial glory.

Disunity and fragmentation were the reasons for the Hindu Rashtra passing into the hands of foreigners. The trajectory was simple enough. First, differences arise. Then, these differences get magnified and a series of dissensions bring about weakness in the form of personal ambition, greed and quest for glory, which inevitably leads to defeat at the hands of aliens. Golwalkar's interest in invoking the historical reasons for the Hindu Rashtra's slavery is hardly academic; it is meant to caution those engaged in efforts to establish a Hindu Rashtra in independent India.

Differences, fragmentation and disunity, he argues, will have to be destroyed. This can be done only if people come face to face with a complete and undiluted idea of the nation. Not only will the idea of the nation and nationalism have to be clear and complete, it will also have to be correct. The slightest lack of clarity or distortion will once again make foreign enslavement a constant and recurring possibility. In other words, a unified Hindu society will have to be fabricated.

In this society, Golwalkar asserts, a moral collectivity will have to be nurtured. Its innermost being, its heart, and its mind will have to be infused with a sense of oneness. This well-established and well organized entity will be a collectivity of every single individual's heart. In turn, hearts will have to be transformed. Character building, therefore, is of the essence. Only that will help create society as an undivided, unfragmented nation. The term Golwalkar uses here is significant. Literally translated, it means creation or composition of humans *(manushyon ki rachana)*. A very strong element of social engineering informs his idea of creating a unified society.

The life of the nation ought to be created, emphasizes Golwalkar, in such a way that human society is self-motivated, self-driven, self-energized and well organized through mutual affection and is also devoid of external controls. Society as the magnified 'self' must worry about the happiness of every individual, and in doing so, create its own life. How is this to happen if there are no external controls? Golwalkar is certain that this could be easily achieved through inculcating in every individual a self-motivated affinity for unity and a thirst for living a unified life. Individuals will change their behaviour accordingly, which, in turn, can be achieved only through injecting Hindu cultural traits into the innermost being.

The supreme manifestation of the idea of perfect unity is to be found in *Advaita*. Golwalkar sees *advaitic* unity as one that glosses over the dualism between light and darkness, capable and incapable, affluent and impoverished, and perceives all these dualities as part of the same substance. Therefore, conflict, opposition and confrontation are part of the same stream of life. This, he says, is the essence of the Hindu way of life and its ideal of unity. It can only be achieved through developing character to a very exalted level, and by inculcating a tendency towards excellence of character.

Once this is accomplished, people would have a sense of *dharma*.[2] Only then would the sense of oneness lead to subjects protecting one another. No external control would be essential. It would be a system based on unity, collectivity, logic and experience. All other experiments that speak of a stateless society have no basis; the Hindu way is the only tenable one. While Golwalkar rarely spoke of individuals living in free India as 'citizens', he often anachronistically referred to them as 'subjects', and resorted to quoting a verse from the *Mahabharata* about a stateless society being one that is circumscribed by *dharma*.

In reality, and till such time as the ancient Hindu ideal was realized, society also had the right to 'oppress'. Expecting anything in return from society or the nation amounts to 'business' and is not 'service'. An individual's concern must only be to do his/her duty and make efforts on behalf of the nation. Golwalkar rejects the idea, for instance, that it is the right of the Dalits to convert to Islam or Buddhism just because Hindu society has done little for them, and they have little incentive to remain part of it. He argues that the only thing those who convert must think about is what they have given to society. They have no business to think of their own selves. Whether society does good or bad, it is the right of society and cannot be questioned. This was also the Hindu ideal of society.

Emasculating the individual further, Golwalkar delineates the Hindu ideal of discipline, without which unity and love of the nation cannot be realized. It grants individuals independence of the intellect, but also demands that there be a rule-governed society, aimed at the ultimate dissolution of the individual in unity and collectivity. The forging of a fine balance between individual freedom and the place of an individual in collectivity is the only way to create a Hindu organization. In a chilling phrase, reminiscent of many twentieth century experiments in totalitarianism, Golwalkar insists that individuals must immerse their ego in the ego of the collectivity. Only this synthesis can bring about unbreakable discipline. This is true in the religious realm as well. Freedom of various forms of worship inevitably leads to one truth, just as water falling from the sky must ultimately reach the ocean.

What is a good example of this form of discipline? Only the Sangh, Golwalkar answers. In the Sangh, people think and they express their ideas. After thinking, all the *swayamsevaks* come to a decision by consensus and proceed to work on that basis. No single individual takes a decision, but in the end everyone's decision is the same. The Sangh is like the answer to a mathematical problem. Its answer, if correct, has to be the same at all times. He cites an instance of Dr Hedgewar, the Sangh founder, being asked why all *swayamsevaks* give the same answer to a question. Hedgewar replied that if they do so, then the answers must, indeed, be the same. In other words, once the *swayamsevaks* are clear about their goal and the vision that informs it, the question of individuality and diversity of thought and opinion does not arise.

Individualism, therefore, is the greatest impediment in the path of devotion to the nation. Society, observes Golwalkar, has become a worshipper of individuals—people either worship themselves or others. The stream of devotion to the nation periodically dries up due to an excessive preoccupation with individual personalities. Even Shivaji, who generated so much energy in challenging the authority of the Mughals and reestablishing a Hindu kingdom, failed to establish a tradition. The need, therefore, is to create a sense of nationalism that is not person or personality oriented.

No durable idea of unity and the nation is possible without awakening Hindu culture. Golwalkar is emphatic that only the sharing of a common culture based on the ancient *samskaras* or cultural memory can bring about unity, oneness and collectivity. When every individual sees himself or herself as a manifestation of that unity, only then will he/she be able to serve society better. A sense of unity and collectivity will bring about a well organized society. Culture is the soul of the nation, and without radically awakening it, a true idea of nationalism is impossible. Character and virtue, without which a nation remains impoverished, can only be founded on culture.

To sum up, every individual has to become a *rashtrabhakta* or worshipper of the nation. For this purpose, every individual has to abandon his/her ego, has to be full of good qualities and virtues, and has to merge his/her individuality in the collectivity.

Golwalkar regrets that ordinary society, as contrasted with the idealistic Sangh, does not think of the nation, and is caught up in the web of self-interest.

Golwalkar's argument for worship of the nation partakes of a historically long-standing tradition of millenarian fanaticism combined with the relatively recent idea of intrinsic superiority of nations and their cultures. God, he argues, is the ultimate unity and is manifest to humans in the form of the nation and its service. The entire strength and intellect of Hindu society has to be placed at the feet of the nation; society's life ought to be run through the nation's mercy and munificence. The nation as God can keep everyone as it wills. It is important to realize that every single body and every life in the nation does not belong to individuals for their use but for rendering service to the nation. This firm belief had been handed down to Hindu society by its ancient thinkers.

According to this way of thinking, the nation has to be seen as one great, glorious, divine, illuminated person, and since all Hindus are a part of it, they must perceive themselves as part of a unity. All parts of this unity are pure and a perfect understanding of this truth would lead to social arrangements that are for the benefit of all. Therefore, except for the purposes of survival, all property and all possessions must be handed over to the nation. The only means available to an individual must be those that keep body alive and life going on. Everything else has to be kept to a minimum. While endorsing Gandhi's ideal of trusteeship, Golwalkar gives the idea a peculiar twist. Whatever comes to us, he asserts, does not belong to us; rather, it is to be presented to God in the form of the nation. If we assert our claims over anything at all, it amounts to stealing from God. This is the perfect unity embodied in the Hindu *sanskriti*: it sees *all* in *one*.

Conceptions of nation as God and as the embodiment of perfect unity increasingly assume oppressive proportions, though Golwalkar took care to articulate it in the language of idealism and moderation. Golwalkar himself asks what would happen if society did not see the truth of nation as God. His answer is that the way to make people see the truth is *danda* or punishment. He quickly adds that the staff or stick, which is the symbol of punishment and chastisement, is merely an outer manifestation of the principle of discipline and punishment. The more viable way to punish and enforce this unity is to enhance one's capability and strength. For the nation to be immortal, it must have power, strength and capability. What is the most obvious sign of strength? To be able to ensure that no foreign attacks take place. Hence, strength is always to be measured in terms of the Hindu nation's ability to take on its enemies.

If the nation is God, and if God manifests himself in the form of the nation, no individual could be greater than society and nation. In this context, Golwalkar strongly objects to Gandhi being called *rashtrapita* or father of the nation. Even Shri Rama was only called the son of the nation, and, therefore, attributing a paternity to the immortal and eternal nation is incorrect. If this is done, it also amounts to an admission that India was not a nation before 1947, and a rejection of the claim of Hindus to be the 'founders' of the nation.

The Hindu Rashtra and its re-establishment, therefore, depend on the excellence and purity of the inner, undivided, man. This task cannot be accomplished by politics. Neither is too great an emphasis on poverty, economic disparities and social inequalities desirable. These are mere slogans and help create further divisions within society. True governance becomes a reality only when all people become pure. But this is a difficult goal to achieve. Until all people attain a certain desirable degree of virtue, it is important to ensure that society is placed on firm foundations. Golwalkar felt that if this is ensured, it is difficult for any system, from monarchy to democracy, to work well.

Politics

In Golwalkar's mental universe, there are two permanent enemies, the Muslims and politics. These two are the greatest impediments in the way of the Hindu Rashtra regaining its power and glory. His argument against politics is articulated at several levels. In the first instance, he observes that if the nation's life were dependent on political power the alien attacks on India would have been repulsed instantaneously. But the Muslims and the European colonial powers came and went away, or lost their power, while Hindu society remained intact. The reason for this is that culture rather than politics informed the basis of Hindu social life. As long as the cultural stream of life can be kept alive and awakened, says Golwalkar, we will be alive. Here, the pronoun 'we' stands for both the Sangh as well as Hindu society.

After the murder of Gandhi and the ban on the Sangh in 1949, there was a clamour within certain sections of the Sangh for greater involvement in politics. The crisis that engulfed the Sangh, it was felt, was a consequence of politics and in order to confront such crises in future, political participation was the key. Golwalkar vehemently rejected this view. He asked those who wanted a greater role for the Sangh in politics to go ahead and join politics. But to argue that there was no worthwhile task to be accomplished other than politics was incorrect and untenable. Politics, he declared, was the most insignificant part of life, and certainly not the instrument that could encompass life. If the Sangh were to keep its faith in Hindu *sanskriti* or culture alive, they had nothing, then, to fear from politics or from those who were antagonistic towards the Hindu Rashtra becoming a reality.

This argument was based on Golwalkar's idiosyncratic reading of history. Hindu society had survived even when those who ruled the Hindus were determined to make the entire nation *mlechha.* During the Mughal rule, there was no one to protect the Hindus and challenge the authority of the rulers. Everyone had capitulated and accepted the authority of the Muslim rulers. Yet, despite force and inducements, the Muslim rulers failed to convert all Hindus to Islam. Hindus survived this onslaught, he argues, because there were people in Hindu society who kept the commitment to Hindu culture intact by singing songs in praise of Lord Ramachandra and Lord Krishna. They kept faith, tradition and piety alive, did not succumb, and retained their moral and ethical voice unto the last.

At any given time, if such individuals are able to keep culture and traditions alive for a period of a hundred to two hundred years, then the cumulative effect of this throws up an individual. Steadfast in his commitment to culture, this outstanding person constructs political power on the foundations of a deep and abiding fidelity to religion, culture and tradition. For instance, from Jnaneshwar to Tukaram, such a tradition of religious and cultural reawakening was fostered, and, in the end, it produced Chhatrapati Shivaji, who established a Hindu kingdom in the face of hostility and adversity.

In other words, if the ruled have unambiguous faith in their culture, then the ruled will ultimately be the rulers. In the present age of democracy, the ruler is not the exemplar of the ruled.

Rather, the ruled determine the actions and direction of the rulers. If the ruled are weak, fearful, untrusting, characterless and full of *abharatiya* or un-Hindu elements, then the ruler will also be the same. These *abharatiya* ideas would be the undoing of Hindu society and the Hindu Rashtra, since these were attracting ordinary people. Political power, however, is not the instrument that would make people worship the nation.

In order to cleanse society of *abharatiya* elements and make people worship Hindu *sanskriti,* it was imperative for the Sangh to enhance its capabilities. Golwalkar is strident in his assertion that every aspect of every effort in the country will have to be coloured in the Sangh's colours. Political power and the government of the day must eventually reflect and radiate the Sangh's light. This could only be accomplished by awakening and disseminating Hindu culture. Neither politics, nor political ideas, nor even sects, denominations and states are eternal. All perish in the ebb and flow of time. What survives and endures is steadfastness in *dharma* or righteousness, religion and rectitude.

If the Sangh's work were to have any salience, if it was to invoke society's faith and trust, and if its voice was not to be dissolved in the prevailing *abharatiya* atmosphere, it had to remain free of corrupting phenomena such as politics and political power. In fact, asserts Golwalkar, the un-Hindu trends prevalent in the country soon after independence were a direct consequence of the quality and nature of political power. Neither political power nor holding political office could help the Sangh's work, or even protect it from any future threat.

Golwalkar gave historical examples of the futility of politics. The spread of Buddhism and Islam, he argues, happened with the backing of political power, but ultimately failed. The political dispensation of the day was against Jesus Christ, yet, because of his faith, his determination and the clarity of his ideas, the Christian faith spread despite the lack of political power. The moment Christianity tried to acquire and align itself with political power and office, corruption crept into its practice. Similarly, those in power at a historical juncture tried to destroy Hindutva in the name of spreading Buddhism, but were vanquished, single handed, by the Adi Shankara. He too had no political power at his command.

The lure of political power and the lure of office had corrupted every idealist, patriot and self-sacrificing individual. The Sangh had to be wary of falling for the love of politics. Rather, it ought to have a comprehensive picture of the nation without giving in to small details and petty issues. It ought to embrace the entire nation in every way.

Politics, observes Golwalkar, is the surest way to lose identity as an organization. Politics inevitably leads to dilution. That might be the reason, he suspects, why Sardar Patel suggested that the Sangh ought to come into the public sphere as a political party and work openly, even if it did so in the name of the Hindus. This happened during the period of the ban on the Sangh after Gandhi's murder. Golwalkar sees in Patel's suggestion a way of ensuring that the Sangh, like all other political organizations, would weaken; and lose its extremism in articulating a radical Hindu nationalist ideology. Instead, the Sangh ought to remain true to the vision of its founding fathers and chart its own course.

With the founding of the Jan Sangh in 1951,[3] the pressure on Golwalkar to delineate a clear line for *swayamsevaks* participating in politics was even more intense. He was clear that the Sangh should have no inclination to leave its work and abandon its goal in favour of politics. But he conceded that incorruptible men could be asked to go out of the Sangh and enter the cesspool of politics. It was not important whether *swayamsevaks* became ministers or not, as long as they had the power and the influence to appoint ministers as a result of their kindness and patronage. The Sangh, then, had to have the kind of power and influence that could run governments and also eliminate governments. Without entering the marsh of politics, the Sangh would have to create a centralized and collectively invested strength in order to ensure the progress of the nation. The Sangh wanted a kind of power which could control politics yet remain untainted by the vices of being in government or participating in politics. The strength that the Sangh envisaged would be able to leave its imprint on politics through its virtues.

For Golwalkar, politics is like a woman of questionable character.[4] Just as a 'woman of the multitude', a prostitute, takes on various guises in order to entice and please, so does politics. A *swayamsevak* in politics is, therefore, like a sage, who, coming in contact with a prostitute, improves her life. The credit, invariably, must go to the sage. Despite faith in the incorruptible character of the *swayamsevaks,* Golwalkar admitted that certain individuals, even though trained by the Sangh, might not ultimately remain free from the poisonous effects of politics. That is why, since the Sangh's inception, there has been a conscious effort to underplay the importance of political and economic issues. The way of the Sangh was one of social transformation and of inculcating virtues in society. The Sangh was in a position to articulate an unadulterated nationalism only because it had refused to align itself with any political party.

If politics was a marsh and a cesspool, then democracy was equally divisive and dangerous. Golwalkar considers the argument that of all forms of government, democracy was the least evil since it promised all 'subjects' representation. In all his pronouncements, he never graduated to the idea of democratic citizens, and never abandoned the idea that nations ought to be run by a handful of wise men and technocrats. His criticism of democracy stems from his conceiving politics as an ongoing tutorial in which perfect human beings are to be fabricated and from his incomprehension of the modern idea of representation, which is based on the existence of formal and impersonal laws and procedures. Therefore, for the success of democracy, he says, it is necessary that common society be well educated. But that is not sufficient. Apart from a good education, they also ought to know economics, politics, and international relations and know these fairly well. Only a well-educated and well-informed society would be in a position to select the right representatives.

If this is not realized, common society will fall prey to self-interest, greed and various forms of enticements, and elect someone incapable. They would, then, have to suffer that individual for five years. What is worse, bemoans Golwalkar, farmers end up being represented by lawyers and doctors, who know little about agriculture. Universal franchise, then, had to be discouraged. Instead, there ought to be a list of all the fields of activity in the country, and representatives should be elected according to these specializations. If this were done, there would be specialists, among a whole lot of novices, to give adequate advice when required.

Neither was democracy a historical necessity. Golwalkar traces the foundations of democracy in the promise of freedom of the individual. Materialism and theories of social contract are the backbone of democracy and the dream of individual freedom. Due to this, self-interest becomes the motive of all action. A society founded on this principle cannot prevent the powerful from oppressing the weak. Similarly, social contract theories are based on the assumption of taking people along, but this is motivated solely by the need to fulfill self-interest and remove any impediments in the way of enhancing one's material pleasures. A society based on ascribing excessive importance to materialism is a *rakshasi paddhati* or demonic system. In contrast, Hindu social life has been harmonious for thousands of years because it is built on the idea of the individual as a manifestation of society.

Further, due to industrialization and some other factors—he does not elaborate what these other factors are—it was evident that the promise of liberty, equality and fraternity is turning hollow. Mutual conflicts become rampant and this leads to the rise of the trade union movement, and soon to the idea of the welfare state. Those who begin with the idea of individual freedom start moving towards greater regimentation.

Socialism's rise is the result of a reaction against the unbridled freedom of the individual. Since individual freedom is seriously curtailed, it comes in the way of the development and progress of the individual. Socialism in recent times has been forced to revert to a degree of individual freedom and allowing some kind of private property. But it has no answer to questions about the quality of man and the forms of life. The only answer socialism has to all questions is materialism. For Golwalkar, socialists are not even humans. On reading an article in *Panchajanya,* where Deendayal Upadhyaya was described as a socialist, Golwalkar says to him, 'How did this happen? We used to think of you as human. So, how come you have become a socialist?'

Communism too is nothing, says Golwalkar, other than an attempt to bring everyone down to one single level. It is a philosophy of 'levelling down' and not 'levelling up'. Everyone has to be kept under the thumb of a central leadership. Added to this is the constant exhortation to revolution, which is nothing but a recipe for bloodshed, anarchy and disturbance. Constant talk of revolution befits dogs, not humans. True knowledge of equality is to be found in Hindu culture alone. Hence, neither of these two systems, Socialism and Communism, is a historical necessity.

What about fascism? Golwalkar rejects as name-calling and abuse the frequent comparisons drawn between the Sangh's philosophy and fascism. He proceeds to analyse fascism, but can barely conceal his enthusiasm for it. The basic idea behind what is called fascism is not so bad, because it is also an attempt at wealth creation and this happens through the primacy and power of society. But Hindu culture has no place for it. Nazism is also a form of socialism. All power and all means of wealth creation are centralized. We do not call it good or bad, concludes Golwalkar, because everything has its uses and can do good in its own place.

Having debunked all forms of political integration and all ideologies, Golwalkar proceeds to elaborate on the only 'ism' he finds desirable, namely, Hinduism. The Hindu alternative was based on the conception of *yugas* or epochs, each of which represented the sentiment in society of the time. Therefore, *Satyayuga, Tretayuga, Dwaparyuga* and *Kaliyuga* each exemplified a distinctive form of society and a unique state. Human selfishness increased in each of these epochs which kept increasing the need for politics and governance. This triggered off a downward spiral leading to a progressive decrease in peace and happiness. The final epoch is *Kaliyuga*, where life is defined by conflict and a struggle for economic, political and ideological primacy. Armies are raised to satiate the hunger for empires. Reflection is absent. In other words, *dharma* is absent in *Kaliyuga* and there is sorrow, poverty and lack of peace everywhere.

Our ancestors, says Golwalkar, did not get fazed or dispirited by the picture they perceived of *Kaliyuga*. To overcome it, they visualized *Krityuga*, an epoch constructed on the efforts of human beings. In this epoch, *dharma* was to manifest itself once again and ensure the happiness and welfare of the entire human society. *Krityuga* cannot be realized through political power or by any form of external control. Rather, it is to be realized through the experience of unity of the entire society, service of the nation, forgetting one's individual sorrows and happiness, and dedicating oneself to one's fellow beings. The sentiment guiding all these actions would be *dharma*.

The idea of *Krityuga* tallies with the modern idea of a stateless society. But the only thing common between the ancient Hindu ideal and the modern concept is that both speak of the absence of the state. Qualitatively, however, the two views are very different. The Hindu ideal of a stateless society is informed by *dharma*. It is important to note that throughout his life Golwalkar uses the term '*dharma*' to indicate a vast cluster of meanings. Unlike Savarkar, he was not averse to the popular and ritualistic forms of Hindu worship, and would often use *dharma* to indicate the devotional side of Hindu practice. In his articulation of *Krityuga*, however, he underplays the external attributes of *dharma* and gives it a philosophical spin.

Dharma, then, is that set of invisible rules on the basis of which the universe does not disappear into nothingness, but continues to exist. These rules get translated into human life, and that too is *dharma*. It is only when humans are able to establish harmony between themselves and the cosmic rules that a stateless society comes into being. This is, however, easier said than done in *Kaliyuga*. Therefore, in order to raise the *Krityuga* ideal, the gulf between thought and action has to be bridged. Golwalkar is clear that metaphysics alone is of no real help. If it were to produce desirable effects on humans, all humankind would become God. Mere dissemination of knowledge does not induce people to accept the truth. Something more potent is needed for achieving people's fidelity to *dharma*.

Golwalkar calls this *shaktipaat* or assembling of strength. The truth has to be conveyed sometimes through example, at other times through touch and on other occasions through struggle. But in order to achieve this state, the material conditions of the nation have to be strengthened and made glorious and capable. In turn, this cannot be realized without recognizing society as one body. The Hindu tradition and its scriptures have described God as one body. Society is a direct manifestation of God and is a mighty leviathan with many mouths, hands, eyes, legs and so on. Also, the way Hindu society is constituted, all its members are imbued with the single consciousness of a single body, and this idea is unique to Hindu society. No other nation in the world has even remotely approximated to this stage. To put it differently, everyone has one body and one consciousness.

At the philosophical level, *Advaita* provides the basis for this radical unity. Having conflated *Advaita* and the Hindu system, Golwalkar argues that there exists a single element that manifests itself in various ways and provides for expression of a variety of interests and natures. However, at a practical level, it is necessary to consider society as a living organism and the human form as the most developed in creation. Only this could provide a durable basis for the composition of society. Put differently, for society to progress, people of the same abilities and similar inner states ought to assemble in order to benefit society as a whole.

For this to be realized, a cluster of capable people is necessary to fulfill the requirements of society and maintain harmonious relations with the entire social entity. These individuals have to understand every need of the living organism called society, and yet have no needs of their own. Only such a group would be able to hold together people as one and run society as a collective unit. That is the reason why the Hindu system bunches together people sharing the same qualities. Golwalkar believes that all human societies will ultimately have to follow this system of harmonizing individual freedom and the need for collectivity.

The caste system in India was the perfect example of such a harmonizing effort. Golwalkar rues the fact that such a fine system was being criticized in the present age in the name of casteism. He admits that the sentiment of 'high' and 'low' within the caste system is not right. But the original *varna* system differentiated on the basis of jobs and tasks an individual performed, which neither created divisions nor made anyone high or low. Had not the Gita decreed that whoever performs his given task would eventually find God? Those who created Hindu society, therefore, thought of castes as mutually beneficial and saw them as part of the same entity called society. Separateness was never a part of the Hindu system. Rather, Christians and Muslims believe that those who did not subscribe to their faith would be denied a place in heaven. But the Hindus never thought of such separateness and distinctions.

In a spirited defence of the ancient *varna* system and its continuing social relevance, Golwalkar argues that the caste system provided a fine balance between individual satisfaction and the need for discipline. This was brought about by people's voluntary and joyful acceptance of roles. Despite all kinds of foreign attacks, it was this system that kept Hindu society alive. The lack of rigidity within the caste system prevented Hindu society from getting fossilized. There is a need now, he feels, to revive this fine mix of flexibility and the imperative of belonging to a collectivity. It is wrong, therefore, to blame the caste system for social conflicts. Historically, no caste had ever attacked another or betrayed the nation on the basis of caste. All distortions within the system were a result of forgetting the fundamental principles behind that arrangement.

There is no need to be apologetic about the caste system. Golwalkar asks Hindus to resolutely assert that there was such a system at one time and it did a lot of good to society. He cites Swami Vivekananda's criticism of many of the ills that had beset Hindu society, but despite these reservations, he considers the four-fold system to be most appropriate and excellent. If society is to be worshipped as God, then all parts of it are pure and the question of untouchability does not arise. There is no need to be apologetic about the past, and the present has to be constructed on this very basis. Efforts by Savarkar and Gandhi to remove untouchability were misdirected and enhanced divisions within society. There were others who blamed the caste system for widespread poverty. The truth was that poverty and deprivation were a direct consequence of forgetting the principles of a Hindu way of life. Untouchability, too, was a direct result of our inability to implement the fundamental principles of Hindu society.

Golwalkar's ideas about the individual, society and politics constituted the bedrock on which his extreme and terrifying vision of the Hindu Rashtra was to be constructed. He believed that just as in the ancient times, seers and sages used to exercise indirect control over politics and society; similarly, the Sangh was blessed with the divine mission of wielding *dharmadanda* or righteous control over politics. Golwalkar saw in modern India a situation where society was bereft of any control over political authority. Diversity and democracy had ruined the unity of Hindu society. In the absence of a clear idea of pure and extreme nationalism, Hindu society was under threat from un-Hindu ideas and forces. Only the Hindu Rashtra could restore Hindu society to its rightful place in the world, and only its ultimate realization would make India truly independent.

In pursuing this ideal, says Golwalkar, a *swayamsevak* rejects the world and all impediments that the world creates for him. Instead, an individual with confidence in the Sangh's work declares, 'I will succeed,' and when he says so, the God in him speaks.

2

We Are Immortality's Children

During Golwalkar's stay in Banaras, a Brahmin cook from Gorakhpur used to cook for him and a few others. When the cook had to go home on leave, he used to say, 'I have to go to my *desh*.' He lived in Banaras, and yet thought of it as 'foreign'. For him, the idea of *desh* or country had shrunk to the limits of Gorakhpur. This innocent use of a colloquial expression to indicate one's village or home rankled with Golwalkar long enough for him to recount it in a speech to the Sangh Shiksha Varg in 1968.

The cook's use of the word 'desh' represented for Golwalkar the loss of the sense of nation among ordinary men and women in the country. Centuries of slavery at the hands of foreigners, he felt, had tied people to petty issues like earning a livelihood. Their world had become limited, and as a result, variety was mistakenly seen as separateness and discord. Golwalkar had lived in Banaras as a student at the Banaras Hindu University between 1924 and 1928, and returned to teach at his old university between 1930 and 1933. India was still under British rule at the time. For a radical nationalist like him, a feeble idea of the nation among the masses during that period was unfortunate but understandable.

In Golwalkar's view, India's attainment of freedom in 1947 did not substantially change anything. The transformation was just cosmetic. The foreign rulers had departed and this led to much rejoicing among the masses, but according to him there was very little to celebrate. Even among the common people who were exulting the overthrow of alien rule, there was little unanimity regarding the substance of the freedom they had gained. A few of them were proud of the fact that independence had been won through non-violence and without shedding a drop of blood. There were others who attributed India's freedom to the bravery and sacrifices of countless men and women. Only one thing united these conflicting voices, and this was the fact of having overthrown foreign rule.

Freedom had left two central issues unresolved. Golwalkar speaks contemptuously of what he calls the unsolved question of relations between various communities in India. Fifty years before independence, he says, an illusion about the unity of Hindus and Muslims had been created. After all, both communities shared the common goal of getting rid of British rule, and this created a deceptive semblance of national feeling. The British had created conflicts between various communities in India, and it would be a mistake to assume that their departure would resolve the tension between them.

The fate of the first outstanding question, namely, the relations between various communities, depended on a second, and more significant, factor. India had attained freedom, he asserts, without developing a sense of pure nationalism. The idea of nationalism and nationhood had not even been born, and people were bereft of a sense of their unique place in the world. Society was disorganized, lacking in knowledge, devoid of hope, and hopelessly weak. It would not be an exaggeration to say, he concludes, that society lacked vitality and was lifeless.

When the Sangh was established in 1925, there were many who were working in the name of the nation without a clear idea of what constitutes the nation. Golwalkar finds the ideas of the nation prevailing at that time inexplicit, lacking in content and misguided. What held these diverse conceptions of the nation together was the sentiment of opposition to British rule. Various political formations like the Congress and the Hindu Sabha were involved in this mission, and so were the revolutionaries. In sharp contrast to these efforts, the Sangh's founder, Dr K.B. Hedgewar, came to the conclusion that an ancient country with a unified past ought to be a nation. He realized, says Golwalkar, that from the very beginning this land was a Hindu nation. An authentic feeling of patriotism could only be built on this basis.

In the absence of a true vision of the nation, warns Golwalkar, it was assumed that all sorts of communities other than the Hindus were also to be part of the nation. In fact, this was seen as a correct and liberal point of view by sections of the Congress and the likes of Nehru. The Sangh's vision, on the contrary, was driven by a singular passion: love for Hindu society. Only the Sangh realized that Hindu society was disorganized and weak. As a consequence it had lost its happiness, and had capitulated to slavery for a thousand years. The reasons for disunity and weakness were obvious.

There was lack of cohesion, and society was fragmented on the basis of caste, codes of purity and impurity, languages, regions and self-interest. Golwalkar ridicules those who looked at the Muslims, who dined together, and had no obvious codes of discrimination within the community, and attributed their strength to these markers of unity. Any attempt at imitating their model of unity, he argues, is a sign of weakness and admission of lack of self-confidence on the part of Hindu society. The solution must, therefore, lie in reviving Hindu culture and forging unity on the basis of culture. Possessing an army, weapons and forts alone had not protected Hindus from being attacked and enslaved by foreign rulers. The need for social cohesion and unity among Hindus was as great in the past as it was after India's independence.

The Congress sought to bring about a simulation of unity that was merely symbolic. Golwalkar ridicules the Congress for wanting to create cohesion and unity on the basis of such external attributes as wearing the same cap and uniform. Even Savarkar, he observes, who wrote such a powerful book on Hindutva, compromised on the question of radical nationalism. The Hindu Mahasabha, under Savarkar's leadership, committed the grave error of passing a resolution in their Nasik session, asking the Congress not to abandon its pure national role by negotiating with the Muslim League. By offering to speak to the Muslim League on behalf of the Hindus, Savarkar certified the impure and muddled nationalism of the Congress as pure. The Hindu Mahasabha became the counterpart of the communal and anti-national Muslim League.

Why did this happen? Golwalkar is clear that the hearts of Savarkar and his followers did not have the purest national *samskaras*. In every circumstance, whether awake or asleep, he asserts, if someone were to ask, 'Which is your nation?', the answer must always be one: the Hindu Rashtra. The Congress did no better. There was a time when Congress leaders spoke of the Hindu way of life with great clarity and sharpness. Some of them even spoke about the ideal of the Hindu Rashtra. Leaders such as Aurobindo Ghosh, Tilak, Bankim and Tagore echoed the idea with force. The Congress platform once resonated with the voice of Hindu India's ancient culture, civilization, history and conventions. But this was a thing of the past. It mattered little to Golwalkar that the inclusion of Bankim and Tagore as Congress leaders was factually incorrect, and worse still, Tagore was never remotely an apologist for the ideal of the Hindu Rashtra.

The new leadership of the Congress had now created a *khichdi* or hotchpotch nationalism in order to please various other communities and to play the game of politics. In its current form, the Congress was wary of using the term 'Hindu Rashtra', and instead was busy creating a jugglery of words like 'Hindustani', 'Indian' and 'Bharatiya' to denote the nation. The national movement, notes Golwalkar, had no conception of what constituted *swarajya* or self-rule and *swatantrata* or freedom. Words like *Ramarajya* were used, but in a way that was tantamount to replacing one meaningless word with another, adding to the already existing confusion.

India was always a nation, argues Golwalkar. To suggest that there was an absence of national feeling before the arrival of the British was, in fact, a ploy to force people to forget their history, or worse still, write a new history that was politically convenient. The wise and the thoughtful had always maintained that this land had a distinctive way of life, which was Hindu. This land has been a Hindu Rashtra since ancient times, he emphasizes. The Hindus were here in this land even before Islam and Christianity were born. This mastery over the nation has to be established once again.

Deeply entrenched *samskaras* cannot be erased, he asserts, by saying, 'Forget history.' In this land, these *samskaras* are granted to us only by a Hindu way of life. The word *samskara* has many layers of meaning. Apart from the more popularly known gloss, indicating rituals, it also means 'impression', 'form', 'mould', 'influence'. But significantly, it also means the faculty of recollection and the impressions created on memory. In another set of meanings, it signifies 'refinement', 'perfection', 'grammatical purity', 'education', 'cultivation' and 'training'. Golwalkar used the term variously to indicate all these meanings, but in this instance, he is referring to *samskaras* as the impressions made on memory by an unbroken chain of shared culture.

The Sangh's founder understood this well. He recognized, says Golwalkar, that the inability of Hindus in the present day to bring a task to its logical conclusion, and their tendency to do the opposite of what their duty entailed was a result of a profound cultural amnesia. The need, therefore, was to ask, 'Who are we, what are we, what is our duty?,' and then provide direction to the common people to prevent them from doing the opposite. There was no difference between death and *vismriti* or amnesia. By reviving the memory of its glorious past, Hindu society had to be saved from self-annihilation.

For Golwalkar, the loss of cultural memory resulted in a deeply fractured identity. The idea that Hindus are the children of Bharat has been attenuated. People see themselves as Gujaratis, Maharashtrians, Punjabis and so on, but not as Hindus. There is no sense of the nation and no pride in Hindutva or Hinduness. Even those who are conscious of their Hindu identity often forget that this constitutes them as a nation and defines national life. Not to recognize Hindutva as the bond of the nation is to invite slavery. It is important to remember, Golwalkar reminds, that the currently impoverished Hindu society once produced Chandragupta, Chanakya, Adi Shankara, Shivaji and Swami Vivekananda.

Golwalkar resents the fact that the moment someone says, 'This is a Hindu Rashtra,' he is branded as being communal and is persecuted. This was the surest sign of mental slavery, especially to foreign ideas. If Hindu *dharma*, Hindu *sanskriti* and Hindu society generate such irreverence and bad faith, wonders Golwalkar, then how can the question of a Hindu

Rashtra arise? Instead, people of opposing faiths and alien communities were being gathered and sewn together in an unlikely quilt called the 'Indian nation'. This was symptomatic of the sway of *ahindu* or un-Hindu ideas, and if allowed to continue, would result in increased conversion to Islam and other alien faiths.

A step towards rectifying this state of affairs, suggests Golwalkar, was to inculcate character and a sense of responsibility among the Hindus. This could happen only if the imagination of nation and nationalism was clear, and if Hindus were conscious of their bonds with it. To know that in the excellence and well being of the nation lies the future of a glorious Hindu Rashtra would be the first step. But the nation demanded unity, a sense of collectivity, love, belief and devotion. The nation was God and every Hindu ought to be engaged in the task of worship of the nation as God.

Having rejected the secular foundations of free India, ridiculed the substance of the freedom won in 1947, and likened the Indian nation, as it exists today, to a patchwork quilt, Golwalkar proceeds to establish the primacy of Hindus in constituting the nation. It was not sufficient to merely assert that the nation was a Hindu nation. A clear title of 'ownership' of the nation had to be restored to the Hindus. This was a matter of great urgency, asserts Golwalkar, because Hindus in independent India, were scared, insecure and did not have the courage to say that this country, religion and tradition were theirs. Such a state of affairs usually had four reasons: ignorance, poverty, attacks by followers of other religions, and lack of unity in society. The last of the four reasons was the most crucial, and if it was handled well, even poverty and ignorance would not become impediments in the way of realizing national identity.

Since the time aliens first attacked this nation, he elaborates, Hindus have tried to establish their rights over this land. Shivaji's efforts were in this very direction. But, in practical terms, while alien rule had formally ended, Hindus were still not sovereign in their own land. It seemed that the efforts of a thousand years had gone waste. During the struggle for independence, people were hanged and shot by the British. Thousands sacrificed their lives and these sacrifices were made by the Hindu society. Despite all this, regrets Golwalkar, political power had gone into the hands of those who short-changed Hindu society in the name of independence and a bifurcated Bharatmata.

Why was the country partitioned? Golwalkar is emphatic that Partition became a reality because Hindus failed to preserve the dignity and honour of their land. They were lacking in strength. Why were they lacking in strength? The sons of this land, he says, forgot themselves and their identity and remained disorganized. Strength gives the capability of attaining and protecting what has been attained. The Gita calls this *yogakshema*. *Yoga* indicates attaining the unattainable, while *kshema* pertains to protecting what has been attained. A disorganized national life does not have either of these two attributes.

Hindu society, warns Golwalkar, must not deceive itself by imagining that since Hindus are a majority in the country, independent India is, therefore, a Hindu Rashtra. Neither should they weaken themselves by arguments in favour of non-violence and peaceful coexistence. These are merely smokescreens to hide the weakness of Hindu society.[1] Rather, they must emphatically claim that the Hindus represent the very roots of this land and they constitute its primary and only component. The very existence of this nation, he adds, is the responsibility of Hindu society. For this nation to survive, flourish and have a fearless life, the Hindus must become sovereign in every way. In this lies real independence.

Rhetoric apart, Golwalkar found it exceedingly hard to answer the question, 'Who is a Hindu?,' and sought refuge in a curious mixture of quirky history and confusing metaphysics. For him, it was necessary to establish the primacy of the Hindus as 'owners' of the nation. Once this was accomplished, he could then proceed to unveil his ideal of the Hindu Rashtra. In taking this intellectual leap, he had to skip a necessary stage, that of even tentatively defining 'Hinduism' and 'Hindu'. Any attempt to do so would unleash what, for him, was the demon of diversity and plurality. If the nation was to be a Hindu Rashtra, it demanded uniformity, unity and collectivity. Unlike Savarkar, who sought to disengage the operative meaning of the terms 'Hinduism', 'Hindu' and 'Hindutva', from each other, Golwalkar chose to live with the contradictions inherent in lumping these terms together.

Establishing the primacy of the Hindus was relatively simple. Golwalkar's story begins a thousand years ago, when, according to him, there was no one in this country other than Hindus. Of course, there were many sects, denominations, languages, castes and kingdoms, but all of these were Hindu. The Shakas, the Huns and the Greeks came, but they had to become Hindus. They failed to contaminate and corrupt Hindu society. Rather, Hindu society managed to absorb them completely. The situation was very different now. Hindus have had to share their land with other religions and communities.

If there are others, wonders Golwalkar, will we be able to 'digest' them? In the ancient world, he says, we had the determination not to allow anyone to leave the Hindu fold. This enabled Hindu society to digest others. But now Hindu society was the object of universal ridicule. This was because there were millions of non-Hindus in India preaching their faith and some had even managed to 'gobble' up a part of the nation's territory at the time of Partition in 1947. After this thinly veiled reference to the creation of Pakistan, he proceeds to analyse the reasons for Hindu society's capitulation to Muslim invaders and its inability to absorb them.

There were people who argued that since God could be worshipped in any form it was futile to object to conversions. If conversion to Islam was solely for the purpose of worshipping God, says Golwalkar, there was little reason to object. But only a mad man would leave the Hindu *dharma* in order to take God's name. The truth was that conversions to Islam had been effected through fear and inducements. When the alien attackers dragged Hindus into their fold, these Hindus, instead of cursing their fate, joined their attackers in what they perceived as their best interests. They accepted their oppressors and adopted their names. Also, Hindu society, he argues, did not have the ability to keep its own people in its embrace and did little when several people deserted it. If this insult to the Hindu land and society was not sufficient inspiration to fight for the restoration of the Hindu Rashtra, then nothing could save Hindu society from further disintegration.

Golwalkar was still left with the task of defining a Hindu. He admitted that people often asked him for a definition of the term 'Hindu'. Addressing the Sangh in 1954 at Sindi, he deftly avoided the issue of definition by resorting to a dramatic rhetorical flourish: 'I say that we are Hindus and whosoever we call a Hindu is a Hindu. Like Jagadguru Shankaracharya, we also have blown the conch shell and we say that whoever hears the sound of the conch shell becomes a Hindu.' On another occasion, he argued that a Hindu started receiving his first *samskaras* or set of values in the mother's womb. From the time of conception to death, a Hindu receives a total of sixteen *samskaras* and these make him a Hindu. Muslims and Christians are born as human babies and become Muslims or Christians only after *sunnat* or baptism.

But when he addressed the Sangh in Thane, less than a year before his death in 1972, his argument was a little more nuanced. Is there anything unique about the Hindus, asks Golwalkar. If one looked at the question of preservation of the self and the species, one would have to admit that there was nothing special about Hindus. As far as the immortality of the soul goes, even Jews, Christians and Muslims believe in it, though Buddhists do not. Again, the idea that if you do a good deed you will go to heaven, and otherwise to hell, is a version of the *karma* theory shared by Jews, Muslims and Christians alike. It still does not mark Hindus as different. Even belief in the non-dualism of *Advaita* philosophy does not incorporate a definition of the term Hindu, especially since the Arya Samaj does not believe in it.

A Hindu is one, Golwalkar explains, who believes in 'our' historical tradition, who reveres 'our' great men, and who has faith in 'our' principles of life. Here, the possessive adjective 'our' stands for Golwalkar's idea of a historically eternal, although momentarily fractured, Hindu society. The new element introduced in this attempted definition is the idea of principles of life. What are these? Golwalkar explains that the assertion that there is one truth which the wise call by different names is an idea unique to the Hindus and is not to be found elsewhere. Further, the Hindus, he argues, think of the inner life without abandoning the world. He admits that Christ to some extent thought of this but claims that Christians do not. And lastly, the concept of the universal soul, the oneness of all being, was special to the Hindus.

There was a simple but significant catch to this definition of who is a Hindu. The universal soul, as Golwalkar understood it, was a Hindu soul, and the idea of one truth a Hindu truth, even though it could be reached through several paths. As long as humans remain humans, he explained, nations and societies would continue to express their distinctiveness. Therefore efforts should be made to bring unity and harmony within the nation and not be mesmerized by romantic ideas of universalism. Only when man becomes overman,[2] says Golwalkar, invoking a chilling phrase from the Nazi period, will universalism become a reality. The Hindus, therefore, had to build a strong national life in order to fulfil God's mandate on earth. There were holy men, of course, who went abroad and spread the message of the Hindu principles of life. But arrogant and insolent people often resisted their efforts. These individuals and communities did not respect words. That is why power was needed to make them see the truth. Hindu society and the Hindu Rashtra were ready to offer nectar with both hands, but if no one was ready to take it, the Hindus would no longer sit hopelessly and purposelessly. They would compel others, for the Hindus knew that everyone's interests lay in accepting Hindu principles of life.

The Hindu way of compelling a person would not, however, be one of coercion. To accomplish God's mandate in the world, Hindu society would have to establish a sovereign, powerful and virtuous national life. This life would be based on the knowledge of the Ultimate, but would also be affluent and materially glorious. Only then would the Hindu Rashtra be able to build on the natural propensities of every other society, inspire them to rise, and leave an imprint of the ultimate truth and good values on them.

Golwalkar would have preferred the term 'Arya' instead of 'Hindu', but he blames the British for having created the poisonous division between 'Aryan' and 'Dravidian'. Elevated individuals in this country called themselves Arya because of their greatness of *dharma* and culture. In the entire world, they were the only ones blessed with character and knowledge. The wise have said that an Arya can never be a slave, whether it is slavery to aliens or to one's own people. If the finest goal to aspire for in life is *mukti* or salvation, the idea of slavery is unacceptable to an Arya. If any form of shackles is accepted, the individual falls from Arya status. This was also the defining feature of what has come to be known as Hindu culture. Freedom from slavery was the natural talent of the Hindus and the mission of the Hindu Rashtra was to nurture it.

While defining a Hindu proved to be difficult, Golwalkar found it even harder to define terms like Hindu *sanskriti* or culture. He admitted that it was difficult to define culture, but argued that the Sangh's work was not affected by the absence of a definition. These were matters best left to debate, and they had no direct bearing on work. Has anyone defined life, he asks, and says that just as the last element of life has been called protoplasm and the matter left at that, so should the debate on what constitutes culture. Many questions arise in the course of life and these are understood through metaphors, elliptical expressions, signs, indications and certain distinguishing features. The best that can be done, therefore, in terms of defining culture is to indicate distinguishing features, signs and characteristics.

The main feature of culture, then, is its existence as a unified, collective body. It is an expression of oneness, which, for Golwalkar, can be expressed in the following manner: I am one, but I am part of a collectivity that takes the form of society. All of us experience a single life flow into us. As an individual, I am here for a few days and it is because of society that I am timeless. My relations with brother, friend and family are entirely due to the life we share together. For Golwalkar, this feeling had to be enhanced, and once this happens, the individual sees inside him the entire nation and sees himself in every individual.

Although he expressed this unusual reticence in defining culture, Golwalkar was increasingly pushed towards offering a more substantive definition. Responding to this demand, he argues that culture is not *sanskriti* alone, and neither is it just civilization. *Sanskriti* is an inner inspiration and has a close association with *samskaras*. Therefore, culture is that generally accepted innate perspective which is self-generated, self-propelled and natural. It is born out of the social life of this nation that has produced many great individuals. Their thoughts, virtues, philosophical insights, experiences and principles of social organization constitute culture. It is the belief system of the nation. It is that perspective which gives Hindus the confidence and inspiration to face the world.

The wars of ancient times were fought on the basis of religion or on questions of ethnicity. They were the glue that bound society together as a unity. Since wars in the ancient past, says Golwalkar, were not fought on the basis of nation states, *sanskriti* was constructed on the basis of religious, political and economic values that were shared by a people. *Dharma* and *sanskriti* alone can, therefore, fabricate a *parampara* or tradition. The nation, whether ancient or modern, was a practical manifestation of *sanskriti* and the cumulative product of customs, observances and collective cultural memories or *samskaras*. The unity of society, then, is based on certain *samskaras*, and the collection of these constitutes *sanskriti* or culture. For instance, it was part of Hindu culture to look at all women, other than one's wife, as universal mothers. These pure *samskaras* were unique to this land and not shared by other cultures whose perspective was lowly and worth condemning.

It would be the task of the Hindu Rashtra to make people worship Hindu *sanskriti*, not through the instrumentality of power, but as a result of the capabilities that the nation would possess. Golwalkar was confident that even those who were opposed to Hindu culture would eventually develop a sense of belonging. Every aspect of national life, therefore, had to be coloured in the hues of Hindu culture by awakening and disseminating its finer refinements. There was just one fear that worried Golwalkar. Within the corpus of Hindu philosophical tradition, there were schools that ranged from preaching pure dualism to pure non-dualism. Even dualism was of two kinds. The *Sankhya* perspective did not entertain the idea of God but on the other hand, there were dualists who believed in God and *bkakti* or devotion. The latter believed that God is separate and different from humans who are a set of phenomenal creatures. Their way was to worship God and live happily. Golwalkar found this position dangerously close to that of Christianity and Islam. Therefore, he warned against this second kind of dualism, where conversion to Islam and Christianity could be justified with the claim that it would not affect Hindu culture and tradition.

The Sangh had sown the seeds for national reawakening on the basis of culture. Golwalkar was certain that this, along with radical unity and an organization based on ethics, would make the Hindu Rashtra a reality. The entire nation would come under the sway of the Hindu Rashtra. But the Hindu Rashtra would not necessarily be confined to the post-independence territorial limits of India. Golwalkar resents the fact that the waters of the holy Indus, on the banks of which the Vedas were composed, no longer flowed in this land. The territories of the nation had shrunk. Post-partition India was not the nation for which Hindu society had struggled for centuries, and it was certainly not the divine manifestation of the Motherland for which Hindus had aspired.

Hindus, argues Golwalkar, were the immortal, divine children of this land. The Rigveda had announced this to the world.[3] The divinely chosen children of the land could not endure its being divided. Nothing but a unified image of Bharatmata or the Motherland would suffice. This would be accomplished by a variety of men. The first category of individuals comprises those that aspired to die for freedom and ended their lives in pursuit of their goal. These were the revolutionaries. There was a second type of men, who sought death after killing a few of their enemies. Rana Pratap belonged to this category. He gave up his life fighting for freedom but did not have the confidence to achieve ultimate victory. The third category of men were like Shivaji. They were inspired by the vision of victory, despite all odds. This was the quality to be emulated in order to realize the dream of *Akhand Bharat* or unified India.

There were people, Golwalkar notes, who considered the post-1947 territories of the nation as a settled fact. However, nothing in the world could be considered a settled fact. To speak in this vein was illustrative of a lack of respect and reverence for the Motherland and for tradition. The very fact that Hindus were alive and lived in the shadow of a divided nation was a disgrace. Even more shameful were the misplaced debates in the nation about the form of the polity and the economic system, while the nation stood shrunk and divided. These trends were a direct result of the continued resonance of *ahindu* ideas influencing even minute aspects of national life like food and sartorial habits.

The nation was the manifestation of the Almighty. The re-establishment of Hindu society as God was the only *dharma.* Golwalkar is emphatic in his belief that everything useful in the task of creating a Hindu Rashtra was *dharma* and all impediments to its realization were *adharma.* There was no difference between the Hindu ideal and the national ideal, both of which were a quest to discover the divine within. The moment the nation approximated to this sense of divinity, belief and piety would be established on a permanent basis. This was not a quasi-spiritual objective to serve pragmatic considerations. On the contrary, Golwalkar believes that all turbulence in the world was entirely due to secularism and the use of religion as a smokescreen for the purpose of increasing worldly pleasures and furthering empires.

The Hindu Rashtra, he argues, did have a temporal manifestation. In it, the conception of one Motherland, one society, mutual interests, similar traditions and the same hopes and aspirations circumscribed the idea of national life. It might seem that the nation was joined together by the force of common self-interest. But to understand the nation's real excellence and its luminous nature was to move away from a merely pragmatic definition of the nation. The Hindu Rashtra, therefore, was the only nation that imparted the knowledge of life's ultimate goal to the world. It was this that made the Hindu Rashtra pure, capable, fierce and radiant. Sages, seers and renunciants, who saved the nation for the last thousand years, had imparted this ideal to Hindu society and their vision continued to inspire nation-builders. They have shown us, he continues, that a strong, capable and glorious nation can be founded only when ancient traditions are made compatible with contemporary times and revived in their pristine form.

The national life of this land was the life of the Hindu Rashtra. Golwalkar rejects the idea that there could be any form of life in India other than a Hindu national life. Despite various differences, sects, virtues and vices, he elaborates, the Hindu Rashtra was an ancient and unified national identity. The thread of culture unified it. Culture was the life-force that inspired national life and the common denominator of the subtle influences and imprints of memory on the heart. Whether people accepted this explicitly or not, or, for political expediency, used a different language to express the same sentiment, there was little ambiguity that Hindu national life was the only reality in India. The Sangh was the only organization that offered a clear, fearless and universally acceptable idea of the nation. In sharp contrast, there were people who entertained the impractical idea that whoever came and stayed in this country ought to be considered a part of the nation. Even to this day, regrets Golwalkar, every alien who settles in this land is deemed to be part of the nation.

Acutely aware that confining the Hindu Rashtra to Hindus alone could result in him being called narrow and communal, Golwalkar preempts such charges as a sign of lack of clarity and residual slavishness. For him, there was one truth and this truth had to be announced to the world loudly and clearly: Hindus represent the idea of nationhood in this country. Whether other communities remained in the country or not was neither his concern nor that of the Sangh. In recent years, the Sangh and its affiliates have argued that the term 'Hindu' indicates a civilizational sense rather than a religious one. This contradicts Golwalkar's clear exposition of Hindu Rashtra and its composition. He was emphatic that the word 'Hindu' was not a generic term. The Hindu society had been sustained since time immemorial by a single source. The social life that was established as a process was singularly Hindu.

In a strident reassertion of the immutability of the Hindu Rashtra, Golwalkar declares that the responsibility for the nation rested on the shoulders of the Hindu community. The onus of earning respect or infamy for the nation also lay with the Hindus. The might of the Hindus alone would determine the power and glory of the Hindu Rashtra. For him, the argument in favour of the Hindu Rashtra was simple enough. It went something like this. This vast land is the Motherland of the Hindus. They are her sons. To serve her is their duty. This land has made it possible for Hindus to have a national life. The glory of this life has to be spread through dedicated service and a sense of duty. Despite differences of languages and customs, all Hindus are part of one society and that society is Hindu society. Hindu society is the only society in this land and of this land. The life of Hindu society is mixed with the soil of this land. The history of this nation is, therefore, the history of Hindu society. Hindustan is the place where Hindus live. This, in turn, means that the life of this country is the life of the Hindus. The nation is a Hindu Rashtra. The Sangh lives and works for the establishment, acceptance and fearless assertion of the truth of the Hindu Rashtra.

Savarkar had defined Hindutva in terms of fidelity to *Pitrabhu* (Fatherland), *Matribhu* (Motherland) and *Punyabhu* (Holyland). Golwalkar incorporates the classification offered by Savarkar, and adds three more elements to it. For him, the Hindu Rashtra was *punyabhoomi, matribhoomi, pitrubhoomi, dharmabhoomi* or the land of one's pieties, *karmabhoomi* or the land of one's actions and *mokshabhoomi* or the land of one's salvation. The Motherland was Bharatmata, and she was the mother of the Hindus. Anyone who forcibly entered her 'house' could not be a 'son' of the Motherland. Golwalkar rubbishes the suggestion that other communities living in the country, given their Hindu ancestry, ought to be considered sons of this land. He sees this as a cynical political ploy to win the votes of non-Hindus. He warns those who doubt the sanctity of the Hindu Rashtra. Those who create impediments in the way of establishing a Hindu Rashtra do so 'at their own risk'.[4] One day, their doubts will be removed and they will be made to accept. Hindustan is a Hindu Rashtra and the word '*rashtriya*' or 'national' is synonymous with 'Hindu'. It follows logically, says Golwalkar, that the word 'national' cannot mean a *dharmashala* or rest house for travellers and pilgrims.

In October–November 1972, Golwalkar addressed the last Chintan Baithak of his life. He had undergone surgery for cancer and was very ill. Neither illness nor intimations of mortality diminished his fervour for the realization of his ideal of a Hindu Rashtra. On the contrary, his last address to the Sangh is unparalleled in the energy, vehemence and forthrightness with which lie advocated the features of his vision. This is our Hindu Rashtra, he begins, and we want to establish its excellence and universally sovereign life. He asserts that the Sangh is committed to this ideal and will work towards it until it is successful. He takes on his critics, and dismisses them as individuals riddled with *ahindu* ideas.

Their main aim, he alleges, is to create confusion about the content of the word 'Hindu'. Inspired by self-interest, these critics blame the Sangh for being opposed to Muslims, Christians, Sikhs, Jains and Dalits. The Hindu way of life and thought, he argues, was present in this land even before Christianity and Islam were born. Therefore, logic has it that the word 'Hindu' in all its inflections could never mean anti-Muslim. The Sikhs and Jains are sects of Hinduism and fall squarely under the Hindu rubric. Even if words like 'Arya' or 'Bharatiya' were substituted for the term 'Hindu', in the end they would come to mean 'Hindu'. Why not, then, use the word 'Hindu' unreservedly, he asks.

The Hindus and only the Hindus can save the nation. Golwalkar asks the Sangh never to give up its insistence on the nation being a Hindu Rashtra. If they did so, nothing would remain of the nation except a flock of two-legged creatures. The argument in favour of the Hindu Rashtra had to be made sharper and more convincing. With complete resolve, the Sangh must say, 'Yes, we are Hindus'. Golwalkar's tone is one of urgency. Be proud that you are Hindus, he exhorts, and say, 'This is my society, my nation and I am determined to make this Hindu Rashtra's qualities stand out and be counted in the world.' If the world wants to clash with this resolve, the Sangh ought to be ready to clash with the world.

If the Sangh were to abandon the historical truth of the Hindu Rashtra and its glory, warns Golwalkar, sentiments like sacrifice, martyrdom and victory of the nation too would disappear. If people still do sacrifice personal comfort in order to serve the nation, it is because they are inspired by the glory of the eternal Hindu Rashtra. The other thing to be wary of is a disjunction between word and deed. Hindu society's tragedy lies in others accepting and working upon principles and ideas that are uniquely Hindu. For instance, missionaries come from countries thousands of miles away, go to the forests, suffer many deprivations, and yet work in order to alleviate people's suffering. But Hindus are loath to even move twenty-five kilometres away from their homes to serve their own people. If Hindus just mouth principles, says Golwalkar, they will soon become objects of ridicule.

Arbitrarily appropriating another set of individuals in support of his utopia, Golwalkar suggests that great men such as Rammohun Roy, Swami Dayananda, Swami Vivekananda,

Keshabchandra Sen and Aurobindo Ghosh had shown the direction of national revival. The revival of *dharma*, he says, was a common thread that ran through their lives and thought. The other dimension of the idea was to make the nation respected, strong and happy. It was, however, necessary to have complete clarity and lucidity about the ultimate beneficiaries of all these efforts. The revival of *dharma* and the glory of the nation was for the Hindus alone. To entertain such aspirations for anyone other than the Hindus was a sign of confusion. Why not the others, some would ask. By including others, the Hindus would lose their identity and the very basis of their existence.

The Hindu Rashtra was the touchstone of national life. While the Hindus had no quarrel with other faiths, no individual or group could be allowed to work against the nation even if such an individual happened to be a Hindu. The examples of Ahilyabai and Shivaji were instructive in this instance. If a person working against the nation happened to be from another faith, Golwalkar says, he too would be treated in exactly the same fashion. Hindus must not hesitate in saying so. He regretted the fact that in free India, enemies were being treated as friends while those who worried about the nation's interests day and night were being banned and restrained.

Golwalkar was once asked if he endorsed the slogan, 'Hindustan for Hindus'. He replied that the Sangh only said, 'Hindustan for Hindus', and not, 'Hindustan for Hindus alone.' He never was able to explain the difference satisfactorily.

3

They Are Incomplete, Uncultured and Demonic

In 1929, Golwalkar went as a research student to the Marine Aquarium in Madras. He wrote a series of letters from there to Baburao Telang, a close friend and confidant. Writing to Telang on 24 January 1929, he refers to a discussion the two had in the past about the question of relations between Hindus and Muslims. Reiterating his position on the topic, Golwalkar says that while there is no need to hate the Muslims, they ought to be beaten up if the time and context demand it. This is, he argues, in consonance with the teachings of the Gita, which encourages humans to rise above anger and hatred, yet exhorts them to fight in the name of *dharma*.

Writing to Telang again on 7 February 1929, Golwalkar curiously suggests that Muslim culture could never be part of the *sanskriti* or culture of this land because Islam originated in a dry and sandy region. He does not explain the connection between this quaint piece of climatic determinism and its relation to Muslim culture in India. He argues further that it would be a mistake to lump Muslim culture and many other cultures under the generic title of oriental cultures. The correct way of typologizing the oriental cultures would be to speak of Indian, Mongolian, Chinese and Mohammedan. Having said this, he goes a step further. The term 'Mohammedan culture', he says, is a bit laughable. Mohammedan culture can be called barbarism, he contends.

In the same letter, he returns to the theme touched in the letter of 24 January 1929. Explaining his position on the Hindu-Muslim question, Golwalkar emphasizes that he was neither against calling Muslims brothers, nor was he advocating that Hindus ought to fight them on a continuous basis. But what if this so-called brother takes advantage of Hindu innocence, if the Muslims call Hindus *'kafir saala'*, and want to dominate Hindus? The question, then, is one of self-respect, Golwalkar clarifies, and of whether the Hindus ought to tolerate such behaviour.

Golwalkar wrote the letters cited above before he had joined the Sangh and developed any association with the Sangh's founder, Dr Hedgewar. But even as a young student, his ideas about the place of Muslims in India were already crystallized. Nothing in later life would persuade him to change his mind about the equation within which he would perceive the Hindu-Muslim question. For him, Muslims would always remain *parakeeya* or those who did not belong. They were enemies who had to be fought and defeated. He did not even consider Muslims civilized. They were barbarians and *raakshasas* or demons.

After independence in 1947, Golwalkar not only rejected the secular foundations of India but also the very fact of India being 'truly' independent. For him, true independence would come only when the question of all alien communities in India was conclusively settled. Only the Hindus belonged to this land, and the eventual establishment of a Hindu Rashtra would bring independence in a real sense. The problem of 'relations between communities' in India, as he called it, had to be sorted out before questions of poverty, development and progress could even be considered.

During the colonial period, the Muslims had taken the help of the colonial masters and had become very arrogant. That was the reason why any articulation of Hindu nationalism, he argued, was seen to be reactionary. After the departure of the British, the Muslims were demoralized and defeated. The Hindus now had to consider whether it would be prudent for them to absorb these aliens into the organic unity of the nation. Do the Hindus, he wonders, have the power to 'digest' them or not? In the early years of independent India, Golwalkar desisted from giving a forthright answer, except to say that the Hindus, who constituted the nation, would have to watch and examine the conduct of all other communities.

The arrogance and insolence of Muslims was a theme Golwalkar returned to with metronomic regularity. He regretted the fact that during the freedom movement, the Congress led by Gandhi had misread the attitude of other communities. They thought that not only the Hindus but also all other communities in India were united against the British. In order to fight this enemy, they sought support from the Muslims. There were others like Savarkar and the Hindu Mahasabha, he continues, who sought the help of the British in order to contain Muslim arrogance and insolence. Golwalkar felt that both sets of people were mistaken because they had little faith in the strength of Hindu society to fight the British as well as the Muslims.

For Golwalkar, national strength and Hindu strength were synonymous. The Hindu nation, he argues, had survived Muslim attempts to convert the whole nation to Islam. There were people in the Hindu nation's history who had held on to the cherished beliefs of their culture and tradition and had thwarted every attempt to defile and destroy the foundations of Hindu society. The Muslim invaders had tried to change the very fabric of Hindu society through force and inducements, but the Hindu nation resisted every such attempt. In arguing this, Golwalkar invariably returns to the solitary example of Shivaji as the symbol of Hindu resistance to what he calls Islamic rule. What is significant in his argument is the idea that all other 'societies' had come to India as attackers and only the Hindus had resisted them.

The British policy of 'divide and rule', he complains, had recognized castes, communities and sects but did not consider Hindus as a group. The leaders of the national movement did not see through this perfidy and sought to forge a unity of all communities, including non-Hindus. In pursuit of this unity, says Golwalkar, the Hindus decided to forget everything, including attacks on their faith, wars fought against foreigners, all the bloodshed and the instances of women jumping into fire in order to save their honour from Muslim invaders. On the contrary, no one dared suggest to the Muslims and Christians that they too should forget their history. What it meant in real terms, he says, was that in order to concoct this brew of unity, the Hindus were persuaded to forget Hinduness, their history, Motherland, their tradition of thousands of years and the brutal atrocities that foreigners had committed.

Golwalkar regrets that men like Gandhi could not understand the difference between a friend and an enemy, although Krishna had adequately explained this to Arjuna in the Gita. Truth, non-violence and the desire to embrace the world, he says, constitute incomplete knowledge. The fallout of this lopsided unity was the pressure on Hindus to forget Shivaji and Guru Gobind Singh and not to sing the Vande

Mataram, as these Hindu symbols of resistance to Muslims might antagonize them. The nation created as a result of these experiments in unity became a *dharmashala*, where anyone could walk in and be considered 'national' just by virtue of living in the country.

In speaking of Muslim arrogance and insolence, Golwalkar detects a dream on the part of Muslims to rule India once more. They were the rulers before the British came to India and they aspired to install a Muslim ruler after the British left. In another instance of arbitrary history writing, he argues that the Muslims realized very early during the national movement that if they remained within the Congress, this dream of theirs would remain unfulfilled. In Punjab, the Muslims sided unsuccessfully with the Germans against the British. Then they ruled, they turned hostile towards the Hindus there and committed atrocities on them. He sees the Mapla revolt (1918–23) as part of the same strategy. In Nagpur too, he continues, the Muslims incited riots and these were stopped only when they were beaten. The phrase Golwalkar uses is *dandey padey* or suffered a beating.

He recollects the trend at the time of the founding of the Sangh. Even those leaders who were loved by the Hindus thought only of the Muslims all the time. The result was that they remained Hindu only in body but their hearts became Muslim. This was not very different from Ravana, Kansa and Afzal Khan and their obsessive preoccupation with Rama, Krishna and Shivaji respectively. In the end all of them had to die at the hands of these very individuals they constantly thought about, observes Golwalkar. Hindustan was the home of the Hindus, he clarifies, and as long as enemies of the Hindu *dharma*, culture, tradition and social life continued to behave arrogantly and insolently in the Hindus' own home, true independence would not have been achieved. It mattered little if the Muslims were originally Hindu by birth. The time had come, he argued, for Hindus to assert themselves.

For the Sangh and Golwalkar, the Muslims posed a greater danger than anyone else. The European colonial masters had left, but the Muslims remained in the country. The first round of aliens came to this land, observes Golwalkar, taking advantage of Hindu disunity. The Muslims who remained in India, he felt, still thought of themselves as victors and rulers. They still harboured dreams of an empire and were bound to make good use of any semblance of disunity among the Hindus. Politicians greedy for their votes were bound to support their cause, and the Muslims, in turn, would make themselves indispensable to any political formation.

Before independence, the Sangh modelled itself as a nationalist organization with a Hindu bias working towards India's independence in its own way. The British left in 1947, and the Sangh was left without an obvious enemy towards whom the insecurities of a certain Hindu nationalist fringe could be directed. After Gandhi's murder in 1948, the Sangh was banned for six months, between February and July. Golwalkar was arrested a day before the ban on 1 February and released a day after the ban was lifted on 13 July. The need to reorient the Sangh's strategy was deeply felt. Golwalkar retained the accent on re-establishing a Hindu Rashtra and sharpened the rhetoric surrounding it. By this time, the Sangh and its leader had found an enemy against whom the putative Hindu Rashtra could unite and rally. The Muslims in India and the Muslim state of Pakistan carved out of undivided India fitted the bill perfectly.

Golwalkar once referred to Pakistan as a *toota phoota ghar* or a ramshackle house of the Muslims. The Muslims had managed to divide the Motherland, he regretted, yet there were still people in the country who wanted to empower the Muslims. Not only did they want to empower them, they also sang their praises and embraced them at the slightest excuse. He found this inexplicable. After all, he argued, the Muslims were no longer just aggressors at home, they also had a country of their own in the neighbourhood that constantly posed grave danger to the Hindu Rashtra. Pakistan would always remain a potential aggressor; to preserve the truncated independence that the country had got and to protect it from external dangers was the responsibility of the Sangh.

The creation of Pakistan was for Golwalkar an act of uncommon cleverness. In many instances, he refers to Pakistan as 'so called Pakistan'. Cutting away the Motherland's territory in the east and the west had created this entity. It was an act of supreme cleverness since the Muslims managed to persuade the leadership of the undivided country to give up their own territory in order to create a nation that would naturally and forever be hostile to the Motherland and its Hindu society. Having created the bogey of constant Muslim aggression both internal and external, Golwalkar was quick to add that the Sangh was not afraid of Pakistan. If it were, it would not have taken the bold step of chanting 'we are Hindus'. It was Pakistan that ought to be afraid of the increasingly consolidating power of Hindu society.

There were many Hindus, he elaborates, who had a presentiment about the birth of Pakistan. Muslim insolence was on the increase in the years leading up to Partition and India's independence. There was a section of Hindu society that had foreseen this insolence turning into attack and aggression. They could sense that the Muslims were determined to establish their sovereignty over some part of this land. When the atmosphere of fear increased, people looked around for protection. They saw the Sangh growing in strength and speaking on behalf of the entire Hindu society. As a reaction to Muslim aggression and the fear it generated, many people started getting attracted to the Sangh, observes Golwalkar.

There was no dearth of people even at that time, he continues, who considered Muslim arrogance as a gift of love and were ever ready to embrace their aggressors. But ordinary people were consumed by fear and were apprehensive. They began to look for ways to secure themselves, and the Sangh provided them that. Golwalkar laments that the earlier situation had not been rectified even after independence. Muslim arrogance and insolence had not ended but people were less aware of it. They did not realize that there was the danger of a real, imminent attack from the neighbourhood. Even today, he remarks, there are people who perceive Muslim attacks and acts of blatant aggression as gifts from God. The Muslims, alleges Golwalkar, did not participate in the freedom movement, and what was worse, did not even criticize the division of the Motherland. Partition brought about displacement of millions of Hindus, but the Muslims never uttered a word against it nor did they do anything to stop it.

Just as Golwalkar saw no difference between the history of Hindu society and the history of the nation, he also perceived this history as one of aggression against the Hindu nation for the past twelve hundred years. The story of hostility against Hindu society had not ended with independence, he clarifies, but had continued in the form of Islamic aggression now being led by Pakistan. These attacks were not merely political in nature but were intended to shake the very core of the Hindu value system. In the past, it was the caste system, Golwalkar asserts, that saved Hindu society from converting to Islam en masse. Unlike elsewhere in the world, Muslims had to make efforts to win over Hindustan. Despite these efforts, only a very small proportion of the population converted to Islam. Their dream of an empire was shattered and the Mughal emperors had to depend on Hindu generals for survival.

It was important for Hindu society to understand that Muslims and Christians were enemies of Hindus. Golwalkar's ire was usually directed towards Muslims, but he often included Christians in his construction of a rogues' gallery. The question of treating them as friends did not arise. Only Hindus, who were the progeny of this land, could be masters of this nation. Muslims and Christians could never be either children or masters of the nation because they were attackers. The Muslims had even encroached on the territories of Hindustan and had cut the Motherland into pieces. For this reason alone, they could not even be considered 'national'. The nation, affirms Golwalkar, had to be clearly and unambiguously Hindu.

Every articulation of Hindu nationalism in the nineteenth and twentieth centuries was accompanied by a caricature of Islam and of Prophet Mohammad. Some of these were elaborate, as in the case of Dayananda Saraswati, Swami Vivekananda and Savarkar. In Golwalkar's case, even the caricature was caricatured to a level of brevity that served his customary rhetorical purposes. He begins by suggesting that Arab society was aggressive by nature from the very beginning. With the birth of the Prophet, he continues, the aggression found new inspiration. As a consequence, they took to arms for the propagation of the Islamic faith, and with that excuse in place started annexing neighbouring areas. Their initial enthusiasm was so audacious that they defeated the Jews, defeated the powerful Roman empire, and installed the Khalifa in Baghdad.

They then moved towards western Europe, winning Greece, Russia and Spain.

They turned their evil eye on India next, says Golwalkar. In this effort, they were helped a great deal by the internal differences and conflicts among the Hindus. Their sole objective in this land was to insult and desecrate objects of Hindu piety and reverence. The Muslims, he asserts, destroyed temples and built mosques in their place, burnt sacred texts, and cut off the hands, noses and feet of sacred idols. Even to this day, after India's independence, they continued to slaughter cows in order to insult Hindu sentiments, though the *Qur'an* advocates protection of cows. Did the Muslims do all this just because they were Muslims, he asks. They did what they did, concludes Golwalkar, because they represent an incomplete, uncultured and demonic tendency.

In portraying the superiority of Hinduism and Hindu society, Golwalkar followed the same trajectory as all other apologists of the Hindu nationalist cause. For him, Islam and Christianity were not even religions. They were just important sects that spread over vast areas of the world in the last two thousand years. The basis of their faith was the idea of one God as father and all humans as his children. Despite claiming God's universal paternity and the brotherhood of mankind, he argues, they failed to conquer the natural feeling of national pride among people in the world. These sects, masquerading as religions, became vehicles for human destruction. They wanted world imperialism of their respective sect at the cost of all other sects, and, in turn, became enemies of the people they set out to conquer and subjugate.

It was not adequate for Golwalkar to portray Muslims as arrogant, insolent and uncivilized. Neither did his argument about Muslims being responsible for Partition and communal riots suffice. In order to resurrect the Hindu Rashtra as a viable entity which could take on its enemies and assert its moral and physical superiority, something more was needed. It required an assault on the aliens, as he called them, at three levels. First, he had to claim that the Hindus had thwarted the designs of the Muslims and fought them gallantly. This meant creating a history that was entirely arbitrary. Second, it was important to portray Muslims and Christians as traitors and enemies of independent India. Third, he was compelled to suggest ways in which he proposed to deal with the inimical residue in a future Hindu Rashtra.

Golwalkar saw Muslims in India as evil, and perceived Hindu society as the destroyer of all evils. All the evil powers in the world that arise from time to time, he says, have been destroyed by the pure life and strength of Bharat. The Shakas and Huns, who harassed everyone, were tamed in the true sense in this land. Islam, which was spreading like a fire in Africa and Europe, experienced a genuine setback only in the land of the Hindus. According to him, destroying evil powers and re-establishing dharma, curbing demonic powers, bringing about prosperity and saving the world were the pure and superior tasks imparted to Hindustan by God.

Every nation, he continues, goes through periods of glory and degeneration. The land of the Hindus too had its share of ups and downs. One such period was when Ravana, the demon king, sought to disrupt all that was noble, good and desirable. In order to restore order and values, Lord Rama had to fight Ravana and bring hope, self-esteem, courage and culture. For Golwalkar, the entry of Islam in India was similar to the disruption of Hindu society by *rakhshasas* like Ravana. Islam had decided to bring the world under its flag on the strength of the sword, and this entailed kidnapping of women, rape, murder and looting the wealth of the conquered nations. The situation in Hindu society, he argues, was ripe for their invasion. Disunity, mutual conflicts and selfishness made some Hindus invite aliens to help them serve their narrow purposes. They could not resist the ferocity of the Islamic assault. Just as Lord Rama was the answer to Ravana's demonic intentions, Hindu society produced Chhatrapati Shivaji as the contemporary equivalent of Rama. People, observes Golwalkar, saw Shivaji as an incarnation of God who successfully vanquished the Islamic *rakhshasa.*

Golwalkar's Hindu history perforce anoints the Hindus led by Shivaji rather than the British as the victors over Muslim rulers in India. Having conveniently skipped a few centuries of history, Golwalkar returns to the question of the place of Muslims in free India. He considers the argument made by many that Muslims and Christians in India were, at some point or the other, Hindu by birth. Their having changed their form of worship, therefore, could not snap their association with the nation and the national life. Golwalkar rejects this argument, however logical it might seem at first sight, and suggests, instead, a proper look at 'history'. Those who converted to Islam and Christianity, he asserts, had not merely altered their form of worship. They had also forsaken their religion, society and national life. They had sided with the enemy and perpetrated all sorts of horrors and cruelties upon their erstwhile community. In other words, they were far removed from any national feeling and had become enemies of the nation. Given such a record, he asserts, it was impossible to embrace them and call them friends.

As if these were not sufficient reasons for treating them as enemies, he continues, they committed the greatest act of hostility by managing to get a separate nation in the name of religion. According to him, the Muslims in India did not see the creation of Pakistan as a final event. Rather, it was for them a first step towards establishing an Islamic empire. Further, they continued to instigate riots and had never assimilated themselves in the national life. Golwalkar refuses to accept that Muslims ever considered themselves part of the national life of this country. They think differently, work in separate ways and plan in different ways, he asserts, and blames them for consigning all non-Muslims to hell. Not excessively burdened with a sense of irony, Golwalkar saw no contradiction in his radical vision of a Hindu Rashtra that conflated nation, nationality and society and defined these exclusively as Hindu. For him, secularism was the rule in Hinduism, but Muslims were communal at all times. A secular Muslim, he emphasizes, is a contradiction in terms.

Just as there was little room for ambiguity about Hindus constituting the nation, there was no place for confusion in Golwalkar's mind about defining the enemy. Addressing the Sangh Shiksha Varg in 1954, he refers to a discussion with Dr Hedgewar, the Sangh's founder, where he was asked, 'Whom would we call a traitor in our country?' Hedgewar clarified that if a Hindu were to go against Hindu society and its way of life, he would be called a *shatrusevi* or servant of the enemy. The examples of Man Singh and Jaichand fell into this category. But those who consider themselves outsiders and attack this country, Hedgewar continued, are not servants of the enemy but enemies pure and simple. Muslims and Christians live in this country in that capacity, he concluded. Golwalkar draws the obvious conclusions from this, and rejects the idea that Muslims and Christians could be servants of the enemy or even *rashtradrohi* or traitors. They were simply not part of the nation and were to be treated as one treats an enemy.

In his 1944 preface to Babarao Savarkar's *Rashtra Mimansa,* Golwalkar blames the Muslims for working relentlessly for some non-existent Afghan or Turkish khalifa. He accuses them of turning their attention to places outside the country and directing their prayers to that destination. Neither do they consider any place within this land sacred, he observes, and concludes that such a community could not possibly be incorporated into the nation. Using a dark and threatening phrase, he calls them *ghar ke baaharwaley* or those who are not part of our home, meaning, outsiders or aliens.

It does not matter, Golwalkar elaborates, whether an enemy is considered a friend or an enemy; an enemy will always remain one, independent of what one calls him. Gandhi had tried to support the Muslims despite opposition from what Golwalkar calls Gandhi's society, meaning, the Hindus. Giving a curious twist to Gandhi's support of the Muslims, Golwalkar implies that the Mahatma supported Khilafat in order to please the Muslims into ultimately helping protect the Hindus. Gandhi considered Muslims to be aggressors in every sense, he alleges, but his way of stating the obvious was different. He cites the example of a Muslim leader close to Gandhi, who later became president of the Congress saying that a Muslim, even if he is the biggest sinner but believes in the *shariah,* is a thousand times better than Gandhi.

Golwalkar considered Christians to be anti-national as well. They too had designs on annexing a piece of territory of the Hindu nation. They preached their faith in the name of religious education, he alleges, but the real motive was increasing their numbers through conversion in places like Nagaland and Jharkhand. They would one day invoke the principle of self-determination and demand an independent state. They too, like the Muslims, were internal enemies.

Despite lumping Christians along with Muslims, Golwalkar was never as strident about Christians, and reserved all his venom for Muslims alone.

All this was by way of analysis. Golwalkar did not, however, stop at just categorizing Muslims and Christians as enemies. For him, the Hindu Rashtra was a reality and its ultimate re-establishment was only a matter of time. In an article written for *Panchajanya* in 1960, he poses a significant question to his readers. When we speak of the Hindu Rashtra, he asks, what do we do with those people who do not call themselves Hindu? His answer to the question is unambiguous: they must call themselves Hindu and must show pride in the Hindu tradition. This means that they can continue to follow the way of Christ and Prophet Mohammad, and need not alter the way they behave in their daily lives. This is *vyakti dharma* or individual duty.

But there was another *dharma* that surpassed the *tryakti dharma*, argues Golwalkar. This is the *kula dharma* or ancestral duty. Muslims and Christians, therefore, must follow the national religion and the religion of their ancestors, call themselves Hindu and behave accordingly. Mere change in the form of worship, he explains, does not alter the national or ancestral religion of an individual or a community. Christians and Muslims, then, must desist from keeping names such as John, Thomas, Ali, Abraham, Hassan and ought to assume names like Rama, Krishna, Ashok and Pratap. To argue otherwise, he continues, is to make a case that the sheer act of going to a mosque or a church makes an individual's blood foreign.

In America, Golwalkar writes, a Negro oppressed by the whites still thinks of his condition as an internal matter. But the Muslims in India, he complains, do not have that kind of patriotism. They have always been in conflict with Hindu symbols of faith and piety, and have invariably seen themselves as victors. Therefore, they would have to be compelled to fall in line and taught a lesson. This required truth, perseverance and courage. The first step in this process, suggests Golwalkar, would be to tell them that their days of rule are over and now they must learn to love this land. The second strategy would be to tell the Muslims that they were once forcibly converted to Islam, and now the days of the sword were over. It was time now for them to accept the faith of their ancestors. Instead of doing this, he regrets, the leadership in independent India was bending backwards to condone destruction of temples, abduction of Hindu women, and so on.

What if the Muslims and Christians were to reject Golwalkar's vision of the Hindu Rashtra and not call themselves Hindu? Golwalkar was categorical that all those Muslims and Christians, whose ancestors were Hindu, must abandon their newly acquired faiths and return to the Hindu fold. Only then, he argues, would independence have true meaning for the nation. If they failed to comply, Hindus ought to follow the example of Vikramaditya. He avenged his father's murder by organizing a formidable army and driving the aliens out of this land. There were other inspiring figures to follow in the matter of dealing with the desecration of the Motherland. Parashuram avenged his father's humiliation by offering him libations of the blood of those who had insulted him. Likewise, the only way to worship the Motherland after she had been defiled, warns Golwalkar, would be to wash her with the blood of those who dared commit such an act.

At another level, Golwalkar advocated the restoration of the old borders and territories of pre-independence India. Only the idea of *Akhand Bharat,* he asserts, would solve the problem of Muslims in this country. It was a problem inspired by politics. If the country becomes one, he argues, the inspiration for Muslim separatism would end and the problem would be solved forever. He was of the view that before the British came and fomented divisions in the country, the process of Muslim assimilation in the national mainstream had already started. Elsewhere, Golwalkar blames Muslims for resisting such assimilation, although if there were instances of such a process, it was the result of the Hindus assimilating the enemy. The examples he gives are of Eknath's pupil Sheikh Mohammad, Raskhan's poetry in praise of Krishna, and Malik Mohammad Jayasi's poetry, which he considered to be better than Surdas'.

At the Sindi Chintan Baithak of 1954, Golwalkar refers to an incident in Nagpur, where he went to attend a meeting called to discuss the question of relations between Brahmins and non-Brahmins. He was surprised to see a Muslim addressing the meeting. The organizers told him that the Muslim was there because Muslims too were non-Brahmins. Golwalkar reacted by saying that if there were differences between Brahmins and non-Brahmins, it was still a question that concerned Hindu society. Where is the need, he asked, to make a Muslim sit on one's head just because of these internal differences. The Muslims, he argued, were not just against the Brahmins but were hostile to Hindus as a whole. Do what you must, but keep the Muslims out, was his message.

Golwalkar found the Muslims and Christians indispensable tools to make the Hindu Rashtra he envisioned, a reality. The enemy was the inspiration. No tangible unity within Hindu society could be contemplated without a call to rally against the arrogance and insolence of the enemy. On the shoulders of the demonic 'other' rested Golwalkar's utopia as also the instrument created to realize the dream of the Hindu Rashtra, namely, the Rashtriya Swayamsevak Sangh.

4

Manu's Fish

Addressing the Sangh Shiksha Varg in 1942, Golwalkar tells his audience the story of Manu's fish. Manu once saw a fish out of water, tossing about in great distress. He took pity on the fish and put her in his water-pot. Soon the fish became large and found the space inside the pot too cramped. Manu released her in the lake, but the fish continued to grow and found even that space inadequate. Manu took her to a larger lake, and then a river, and finally to the ocean. At the time of the dissolution of the world, Manu saved himself on the back of the fish. After the catastrophe settled down, Manu recreated the universe. The Sangh, Golwalkar concludes, was growing like the mythical fish and was ready to save Hindu society and the world from dissolution and danger. All that was needed was organizing Hindu society, empowering it and establishing the unambiguous claims of Hindus over the nation.

Golwalkar never doubted that the Sangh was God's mission on earth. It was, however, not an ordinary mission. In invoking a fraught and emotionally charged image of the Sangh, he once described it as God's incarnation in the world to end *adharma*. God manifests himself sometimes in human form and at other times in the form of an organization. In *Kaliyuga*, the highest form of strength was organization. God, then, had manifested himself in this day and age in the form of the Sangh in order to organize *samskaras.* No one else had thought of the nation in terms of passing on a legacy of eternal values from generation to generation. Only the Sangh had taken upon itself this role of strengthening the nation on the basis of disseminating values. This was the Sangh's mission, according to Golwalkar.

The Sangh's pledge and aim were tailored accordingly. Delineating these in the clearest terms, Golwalkar saw the Sangh as an instrument for the spread of knowledge of *dharma* and *sanskriti.* The organization ought not to confine itself, he felt, to any preoccupation with forms of external progress and material development of the nation alone. Rather, it ought to cater to the inner realm of individuals. It was not the business of the Sangh to worry itself about solving current problems. This was the reason, he explained, why the Sangh continued to do its own work rather than participating in the crucial moments of the freedom movement in 1930–31 and then in 1942. The Sangh envisaged the creation of an entity called 'Hindu society' as more crucial than any other task. This could only be done when every heart in the country entertained the idea of a pure unity based on mutual affection, and moved towards a situation where the entire society became 'one heart'. Golwalkar calls this the 'condition precedent'[1] of the Sangh.

Golwalkar interpreted Hedgewar's vision in founding the Sangh as one of creating an independent, well-established tradition that was Hindu in orientation, working for the autonomy of Hindu society, and with the aim of making the entire world bow before the power and glory of this Hindu consolidation. Therefore, the operative lines in the Sangh's pledge were: 'To make the Hindu Rashtra independent by protecting Hindu *dharma,* Hindu *sanskriti* and Hindu society.' In the early days of the Sangh, Hedgewar had hoped that in fifteen years, the work of the Sangh would reach a critical mass. He died soon after the completion of those fifteen years. In his last days, says Golwalkar, the target was reset to extend by another three years. He planned that in these three years 1 per cent of the entire population in rural areas and 3 per cent of the total population in urban areas ought to be transformed into dedicated *swayamsevaks*. He dreamed of creating a band of young, committed, uniformed, aware and enlightened *swayamsevaks*. Golwalkar regrets that the Sangh did not take his vision seriously enough, and it was this that led to the upheavals of 1942 and the subsequent partition of the country.

As early as 1939, Golwalkar was casting the Sangh in patently Hindu colours. In a speech in that year, he compared the act of joining the Sangh to a second birth. In doing so, an individual ceases to be an animal and becomes human. The term he used is '*dwija*', and though he translates it literally as 'second birth', the obvious and popular gloss of the term to connote a Brahmin could hardly be lost on anyone. In 1951, he further refined this typology by suggesting that Brahminhood was the Sangh's inspiration and Kshatriyahood its strategy. Not only was the Sangh an incarnation of God, it was the only *shastra* or scriptural authority that he and other *swayamsevaks* recognized.

Neither was the Sangh a mass movement. Golwalkar rejects the idea of converting the Sangh into a mass movement, arguing that mass movements were only capable of destructive work. Quoting Mark Antony in Shakespeare's *Julius Caesar*, he condemns mass movements as good only for rousing the masses, but not for national reconstruction of the kind he envisaged. He was generally averse to any form of struggle, violent or non-violent, arguing that any form of fight left behind scars and distortions, and disrupted the rules of social formation. The Sangh was, he asserts, a 'class' movement, not in the Marxist sense, but in terms of creating a disciplined and powerful organization on the basis of values. The Sangh was to him a *mahayantra* or great instrument. Its virtuous members had drunk the nectar of organized life. Coercion alone could not make humans comply; for them to see themselves as part of a nation ought to be the outcome of an idea that truly inspires.

The reason the phrase 'Hindu sanskriti' is used in the Sangh's pledge, elaborates Golwalkar, is to create an unadulterated, unambiguous and dynamic idea of the nation. This objective would remain largely unaccomplished in the absence of purifying, elevating and clarifying the ideas of nation and nationalism on the basis of culture. Whatever was inherent and excellent in Hindutva had to be re-established on the basis of uniting all Hindus in a bond of love, destroying all divisive forces within Hindu society and making all members of Hindu society realize their shared tradition. All external differences within Hindu society, he further argued, were mere shadows. Only mutual love, faith and respect among all sections of Hindu society would eventually translate into reverence and love for the Motherland. The Sangh, he concluded, had taken upon itself to sow the seeds of pure national character, selfless social service, duty and knowledge of unity among all sections of Hindu society.

The Sangh's identity was therefore confined to the affirmation of the dictum, 'We are Hindus', and was not circumscribed by external symbols. Golwalkar was strident about this aspect of the Sangh's identity. A transformation in behaviour and attitude, he asserted, was a greater symbol than a cap or a flag. It also helped the Sangh avoid assuming the character of a sect or a political formation. What, then, was the purpose of the Sangh beyond the creation of a Hindu Rashtra through cultural awakening? Golwalkar's answer places him in the forefront of modern demagogues. For him, constitutional niceties were the business of politicians. The Sangh, he argued, was engaged in the qualitative task of establishing a controlled and regulated body that exuded power. It was to be a controlled work force, not one that rouses the anger of people, but one that could do so effectively when the need arose. It was to be so perfectly controlled and all-powerful that it could also control the anger that it had generated.

In the same breath, Golwalkar was quick to clarify that the strength of the Sangh came not from its role of protecting Hindus against the Muslims but from educating people about *Bharatvarsh*, an individual's place in it, and the place of *Bharatvarsh* in the world. The Sangh's goal was to create a form of nationalism that was not beholden to individuals. Rather, it had to fabricate a society where individuals dissolved themselves in perfect unity, in order to express a pure love of the nation. The Sangh's inspiration, he explains, was the Motherland below, God's sky above, and the Hindu society spread all across the land. This inspiration was best symbolized by the game of *kabaddi*. It represented the inextricable link between the assertion of Hindu identity and the Motherland. According to him, *kabaddi* brought people together and fostered affection. He gives the instance of an unlettered *swayamsevak* going to a certain place with just the knowledge of the fundamental tenets of the Sangh: love of the Motherland, pride in his Hindu identity, and Hindu consolidation through affection and organization. He was asked to enter into a debate with someone. Instead, the *swayamsevak* suggested that this gentleman play *kabaddi* with him for a week and then enter into a debate. After a week, *kabaddi* had infused an atmosphere of affection and had ensured that all arguments and questions vanished. Golwalkar felt that *kabaddi* managed to bring people together more effectively than ambitious plans and strategies.

Golwalkar was acutely conscious of the discomfort among many in the Sangh about the organization's indifference to economic and political issues. He answers these elements within the Sangh by reminding them that from the time of its inception, the founders of the Sangh had consciously decided to stay aloof from these issues. To capitulate to short-term goals would be to be infected by the race for power and position seen all around. Neither should the Sangh assume that it was best suited for office because of its organizational discipline and emphasis on purity of character. The Sangh's ideal, he emphasizes, was that of renunciants, who stay aloof from power, but step in to hold the reins of authority at times of crisis. The Sangh's primary objective was to remove vices from and develop requisite virtues in Hindu society. Success in this task alone, he asserts, was the measure of the Sangh's achievement. The aim was to create a tradition of effort on the basis of unity and collectivity.

Rhetorical allegiance to unity was one thing, but to run an organization was another matter altogether. Golwalkar struggled all his life with the threat of common human frailties and foibles disrupting the way he sought to mould the Sangh. He admitted that selfishness, individual opinions and the inability to persuade were impediments in the way of collective effort, and pleaded for *swayamsevaks* to work through affectionate persuasion and through mutual consultation. He was conscious that despite talking about ideals, many within the organization fell short of implementing these in their own lives. In organizational matters, he wanted the Sangh and its members to abandon rigidity and become 'realists' like him. Just as inculcating good character was of paramount importance for the nation as a whole, so was it for the organization. But character had to be pure in the personal realm as well as in the social arena. Otherwise, the exclusion of one in favour of the other, he notes, would push the Sangh and its members towards the ills that beset Western societies, where only social duties were emphasized to the detriment of personal ones.

It was important, Golwalkar argues, that every individual associated with the Sangh become better. As a first step, this individual's knowledge must be enhanced, along with patriotism and a clear idea of the nation's history, ideals, and goals. The Sangh, he elaborates, must inculcate in every person the sense that a better life comprises the feeling of unity from within, purity of behaviour, and ideas of greater brotherhood and social unity. In developing these feelings, an individual would be able to take on the burden of the entire organization on himself and run it smoothly. The Sangh's programmes, insists Golwalkar, must make an impact on the body, heart and mind. If worship of idols, singing hymns, prayers, pilgrimage, yajna and other rituals help in harnessing the inner sentiments of an individual, these ought to be encouraged.

The strategy of the Sangh had to also take into account the fact that even within the so called Hindu society, as it sought to define it, there was little enthusiasm for what Golwalkar termed 'militant nationalism'. Acutely aware of the danger of members of the Sangh beginning to exhibit a sense of moral superiority over the rest of society on account of their allegiance to militant nationalism, Golwalkar appealed to members to be modest. The idea of the assertion of a militant Hindu nationalism was the Sangh's gift to Hindu society, and it was premature to expect every Hindu to cherish a vision of selfless devotion to the nation. He admitted that the rest of society, barring the Sangh, was leading a low life and had lost touch with all forms of excellence, but this was no reason for the Sangh to exclude them from its sphere of influence. The ancient sages, he argues, called themselves Arya and thought of all others as *mlechha.* But even they did not rule out the possibility of the *mlechhas* getting a glimpse of the divine. Therefore, it was imperative for the Sangh to make everyone welcome and hold society together without compromising on self-respect. The goodness in everyone, he suggests, ought to be enhanced, while all flaws could be removed through tact, intelligence, mutual affection and love. If Hindu society was a manifestation of God, and if God made no distinction between high and low, wise and foolish, then the same rule applied to the Sangh, he concluded. Golwalkar meant this lesson in modesty, in the first instance, for *swayamsevaks.* He feared that they might become pompous, self-righteous and sanctimonious in relation to other Hindus who were not within the Sangh fold. It was also a strategic move to help ensure that the rigid code of the Sangh did not alienate potential entrants.

Golwalkar implores *swayamsevaks,* then, to consider themselves servants of Hindu society and make *seva* or service the benchmark of all their efforts. They were to take pride in this sense of dedication to society and its service alone. Complete dissolution of the self in work would move all forms of petty distraction away from them. There was no place within the ambit of the Sangh's discipline for individual choice or wishes. It was incumbent upon a *swayamsevak,* reminds Golwalkar, to give everything up for the sake of the Sangh. Nothing other than the Sangh mattered, not wife, child, money or family. He usually held Dr Hedgewar up as an exemplar of complete devotion and sacrifice.

The Sangh's discipline was supreme. Orders, especially of superior individuals, had to be followed under any circumstances. He gives an interesting example of the crucial role discipline played in the Sangh's scheme of things. Dr Hedgewar and Golwalkar were travelling in 1938 to Lahore. A Sangh worker folded a blanket for the journey and started packing it inside a holdall. The holdall was broad, but the worker had folded the blanket in such a way that it created an awkward lump when the holdall was tied. Hedgewar tried to show the worker the correct way of folding the blanket, but that individual remained stubbornly unconvinced. Golwalkar then tried to fold the blanket correctly and Hedgewar did not comment on his effort. Golwalkar thought that the Sangh founder had remained silent out of deference to him. But when the worker later asked him the difference between the two attempts at folding the blanket, Hedgewar pointed out his error to him. Even small acts of noiselessly closing a door or folding a blanket, Golwalkar observes, were part of the cumulative and non-negotiable discipline of the organization. The strength, longevity and very survival of the Sangh, he concludes, depended on the voluntary acceptance of the discipline of the organization by individuals who were vital and radiant.

One of the most striking features of Golwalkar's vision of the Sangh is his description of the life of a *swayamsevak*. Not only is it distinctively authoritarian in terms of organizational discipline, it also reflects the way in which a certain reading of the notion of renunciation was grafted on to the Sangh. From the outset, Golwalkar makes it clear that the entire life of a *swayamsevak* belonged to the Sangh and its work. Therefore, there was no question of entertaining any thoughts about wanting a family life. He expresses surprise at the yearning for a family, and suggests that this wish could be fulfilled in another lifetime while this life ought to be dedicated to completing the work that the Sangh had undertaken. He cites the example of a conversation between Hedgewar and a friend. The friend said that in life it was possible to have only one friend, while all others are mere acquaintances. Hedgewar retorted that if the friend were to get married, his one friend would be his wife, while all other Sangh workers would be reduced to acquaintances. With a touch of sarcasm Golwalkar observes that this friend eventually married, and faithfully served his only true friend, namely, his wife.

The ordinary and well-regulated life, then, was not for the Sangh. Golwalkar wonders how the inheritors of the glorious Hindu tradition could reduce themselves to being born, growing up, acquiring an education, getting married, producing children, growing old and finally dying. Everyone does this, he says, even plants follow a similar trajectory. The *swayamsevak* ought to be free of such ephemera. Moreover, there was a real danger in getting married, says Golwalkar. An individual who remains in touch with a woman, even if she is his wife, or thinks constantly of his wife, takes on feminine characteristics.[2] This, in turn, alienates him from the Sangh's work, which is masculine.

Neither should *swayamsevaks* worry about old age, he continues. There were several individuals who worried excessively about impending decrepitude and infirmity, and felt that the Sangh ought to take care of them in old age. Golwalkar dismisses this worry as selfishness, and suggests that these people ought to leave old age to take care of itself. He does not stop at this. In what follows, Golwalkar outlines the most heartless and ruthless guidelines for the ideal *swayamsevak*. These were delivered in March 1954 at the Sindi meeting. A full paraphrase of Golwalkar's speech is reproduced here:

- I have said many times that as long as this body can do the Sangh's work, it is all right.
- The day doing the Sangh's work becomes impossible, the body must pass on, it must not remain.
- If the body refuses to pass on, leave it on the roadside, but do not become a burden on the Sangh.
- We are here to look after our work, and even if we have given our lives to it, we must have no reciprocal expectations from the organization.
- There is an idea of business or trading behind the sentiment of expectation, and it dilutes pure devotion to the organization. There can be no trading with the Sangh's mission and its goal.
- The way the Sangh keeps you, you will remain. If it kills, you will die.
- You will not even ask, what did I do to deserve this? You must not even entertain this thought.
- You must say: 'The way the Sangh keeps me, I shall remain.' From within your inner being, you must abandon the idea of choosing your life. The individual who conquers his heart destroys stray thoughts as well.
- If an individual decides to have choices within service, then it is no *seva* or service. It is merely employment.
- Even within the Sangh, one must abandon the idea of choice in terms of areas of work. That too becomes employment, even if it is non- remunerative employment.

If all *swayamsevaks* were to be moulded according to Golwalkar's severe vision, then a band of dedicated *pracharaks* had to be created. These men would emulate the fullness of the Sangh's objectives and follow the discipline envisaged by the organization. Dearth of dedicated *pracharaks* was a real issue for Golwalkar. He constantly raised the issue in all his public pronouncements. He spoke of the need for *pracharaks* who would employ all their life, time, energy, intellect and feeling in the Sangh's work and think of little else. Another article of faith was the primacy of the *shakha*. Golwalkar saw the *shakha* as Hedgewar's finest invention. He perceived it as a form of daily worship, where values were inculcated, and advocated great firmness in ensuring attendance at the *shakha*. The example he gave to impress upon the need for regularity in coming to the *shakha* was that of a peacock who strayed into a rich man's garden. This man wanted the peacock to come to his garden regularly, so he began feeding the bird opium balls. Slowly, over a period of time, he withdrew the feed, but the peacock still came to the garden regularly. The bird continued to come, surmised Golwalkar, because it had formed a habit.

It is commonplace even today for the Sangh to profess a lofty disinterest in politics. The rhetoric to this day is one of organizing Hindu society and inculcating values and cultural re-awakening, with the ultimate goal of establishing a Hindu Rashtra. This is the logical completion of the 'work', as the Sangh chooses to call it. However, for Golwalkar, the 'work' had two distinct dimensions. The first, he elucidates, was to reach every individual in Hindu society and transform their hearts for the purposes of building a collectivity. This was the logical completion of the Sangh's 'work'.

There was, however, another significant gloss to the term 'completion of goal'. It places out in the open the Sangh's hidden aspiration for power while appearing aloof and disdainful of politics. The ability to affect and control every dimension of society was the other inflection to the term 'completion of goal'. The 'work', argues Golwalkar, had to become vast and all-embracing in order to enable the Sangh to have lordship over the minds of the masses. He argued fervently for the need for power, without which the 'work' would end in failure. One must be effective and influential in order to do anything, he observes. Golwalkar envisaged a day when politics and government would eventually take orders from the Sangh. This could happen only if the rules of the Sangh's mission and strategy were followed diligently.

Turning to the question of 'inspired' organizations, like the Jan Sangh, Golwalkar characterizes them as additions to the Sangh's work rather than substitutes. The Sangh's relationship with them was the same as Lord Krishna's with existence, as explained in the Gita: I am in all that exists and they are in me, but I am not in them and they are not in me. A sick man can be given porridge as food, he further elaborates, but a healthy man cannot be fed porridge in place of normal food. Instead, a healthy man can eat porridge with his normal diet. Similarly, the Jan Sangh had not come into existence to rectify some deficiency within the Sangh nor was its work that important as to be worth reducing the Sangh's activities. The Jan Sangh worked in the political field in order to bring pure ideals into practice and conduct itself in a manner that was above mutual jealousies and competition. The Jan Sangh, he continues, existed in order to establish the primacy and importance of the Sangh in the political field. In fact, the Sangh would eventually be able to direct the entire process of governance through the Jan Sangh.

Golwalkar was clear that *swayamsevaks* 'given' to the Jan Sangh were expected to conduct themselves in the same way as they did in the Sangh, and as was expected of *swayamsevaks.* They ought not to delude themselves with the thought that they were free, he warned. They were not expected to beat their own drum, get a name for themselves and lead the rest of their lives in peace and prosperity. If the lure of politics made these *swayamsevaks* forget the ideals of the Sangh, they would do the Sangh and the nation great harm. All members of the Jan Sangh, he clarifies, were the Sangh's ambassadors. Just as an ambassador does not land in another country and promptly get married in order to settle down on foreign soil, the same was true of members of the Jan Sangh. Neither should *swayamsevaks* working in the Jan Sangh forget the parent organization's modes of worship. This meant that they had to regularly attend *shakha.*

Dispelling any ambiguity that might remain, Golwalkar clarifies that *swayamsevaks* in the Jan Sangh had not been sent there to do the Jan Sangh's work. They were there to enhance the Sangh's influence in the political arena. The bond with the Sangh had to remain unaffected by any amount of political work. Rather, it was incumbent upon the Jan Sangh to help in pushing and expanding the Sangh's agenda. Wherever a *swayamsevak* works, he ought to establish the Sangh's ideals there and make that arena of activity a 'recruiting ground'[3] for the Sangh. The commander-in-chief fights the battle, says Golwalkar, but the credit invariably goes to the leader who sent him. A time must come, he contemplates, when it would be possible to state that the Sangh *is* the Hindu Rashtra. This was the second layer of meaning Golwalkar imparted to the phrase 'completion of work'.

In the course of articulating the vision and strategy of the organization, Golwalkar was only too conscious of the limitations of the Sangh. He spoke about the gulf within the Sangh between lip service to normative ideas and actual practice; he attributed this gulf to the lack of development of inner qualities. The Sangh, he maintained, was the only organization that imparted *samskaras* or values. If there were obvious failures, these were not because of a flaw in the path chosen but due to lack of effort. Its failure in capitalizing on the growing cynicism in society was only one instance of the absence of a concerted strategy to turn such phenomena into an advantage for the Sangh. He quotes Hedgewar who believed that no external threat could harm the Sangh. Rather, the *swayamsevaks*, through their vices, would be in a position to destroy it. They were active and dutiful, but these virtues could also be diverted into creating harmful values.

Like most angry prophets, despots and messianic fanatics, Golwalkar believed in the ultimate triumph of his vision. He saw the Sangh as God's chosen instrument in re-establishing the imagined Hindu Rashtra. No element of doubt or diffidence ever marred his belief in the rightness of his cause. He perceived the Sangh as a non-threatening organization, yet in the same breath would talk about attack as the best form of defence of the Hindu Rashtra. In fact, he saw the 'work' itself as a preparation for attack rather than defence. Yet, on other occasions, he would quote Hedgewar and argue that the Sangh was neither scared of anyone nor did it intimidate anyone.

What best exemplifies the Sangh is Golwalkar's insistence that it was not answerable to anyone. At one level, this betrays a degree of smug confidence in one's own deeply cherished pieties, but on the other hand it reflects the organization's lack of accountability and aversion to any form of discussion and debate. Addressing a gathering at Sindi in 1954, Golwalkar dismissed the idea that the Sangh's survival was contingent upon the blessings of the government or anyone else. It is unstoppable, he declared. Quoting Hedgewar again, Golwalkar declared that the Sangh was not answerable to anyone and was not obliged to answer its detractors. When the need arises, he said, we will reply. He dared critics to pass resolutions, write what they felt like and say what they wished. All these criticisms were to be countered with silence. Answering one's detractors, he affirms, enhances their strength. Silence wards off many problems. What mattered was faith in the 'work' and the creation of the Hindu Rashtra.

Notes

Introduction

1. For Golwalkar's life, see C.P. Bhishikar, *Sri Guruji: Pioneer of a new era*, Sahitya Sindhu Prakashan, Bangalore, 1999; Walter K. Andersen and Sridhar Damle, *The Brotherhood in Saffron: The Rashtriya Swayamsevak Sangh and Hindu Revivalism*, Westview Press, Boulder and London, 1987; *Sri Guruji Samagra*, vols. 1, 6 and 12, Dr. Hedgewar Smarak Samiti, Nagpur, 2005.
2. For a fuller account of the ban on the Sangh, see Walter K. Andersen and Sridhar D. Damle, The Brotherhood in Saffron: The Rashtriya Swayamsevak Sangh and Hindu Revivalism, Westview Press, Boulder and London, 1987, pp. 50–55.
3. Gwilym Beckerlegge, *Swami Vivekananda's Legacy of Service: A Study of the Ramakrishna Math and Mission*, Oxford University Press, New Delhi, 2006, pp. 192–200. Also see, Gwliym Beckerlegge, 'Saffron and Seva: The Rashtriya Swayamsevak Sangh's Appropriation of Swami Vivekananda', in *Hinduism in Public and Private: Reform, Hindutva, Gender, and Sampraday*, edited by Anthony Copley, Oxford University Press, New Delhi, 2003, pp. 31–65; Gwilym Beckerlegge, 'The Rashtriya Swayamsevak Sangh's 'Tradition of Selfless Service', in *The Politics of Cultural Mobilization in India*, edited by John Zavos, Andrew Wyatt, Vernon Hewitt, Oxford University Press, New Delhi, 2004, pp. 105–135.

4. *The Call of the Spirit: Conversations with Swami Akhandananda*, Sri Ramakrishna Math, Madras, 1984, p. 92.
5. Ibid., p. 99.
6. Gwilym Beckerlegge, 'Saffron and Seva: The Rashtriya Swayamsevak Sangh's Appropriation of Swami Vivekananda', in *Hinduism in Public and Private: Reform, Hindutva, Gender, and Sampraday*, edited by Anthony Copley, Oxford University Press, New Delhi, 2003, pp. 31–65.
7. Jyotirmaya Sharma, *Hindutva: Exploring the Idea of Hindu Nationalism*, Penguin/Viking, New Delhi, 2003.
8. *Sri Guruji Samagra*, vol. 6, p. 178.
9. Ibid., p. 178.
10. Ibid., p. 211.
11. Ibid., pp. 216–7.
12. Ibid., pp. 225–7.
13. Ibid., pp. 244–5.
14. Ibid., p. 249.
15. Ibid., pp. 250–6.
16. Ibid., pp. 265–6.
17. A thoughtful commentator like G.P. Deshpande (GPD), writing in the *Economic and Political Weekly* of March 25, 2006, p. 1165, writes: 'His theoretical or ideological legacy is made of two books. One is his *Bunch of Thoughts* and the other is *We or Our Nationhood Defined*.'
18. See a fuller discussion on this issue in Chapter 1. V.D. Savarkar's older brother, Ganesh Damodar Savarkar alias Babarao Savarkar, originally wrote the book. This book has now been formally withdrawn as part of Golwalkar's works, though his foreword to the volume still appears in vol. 6, p. 109, of his complete works, published in 2005.
19. *Shri Guruji Samagra*, vols. 1–12, Dr. Hedgewar SmarakSamiti, Nagpur, 2005.
20. *Shri Guruji Samagra Darshan*, vols. 1–7, Bharatiya Vichar Saadhana, Nagpur, 1978.

21. The constitution of the Rashtriya Swayamsevak Sangh was adopted on 1 August 1949 and amended on 1 July 1972.
22. The Sangh calls its affiliates 'inspired' organizations.
23. *The Constitution of the Rashtriya Swayamsevak Sangh*, Article 3.
24. There is considerable literature on this topic. See P.J. Marshall (ed.), *The British Discovery of Hinduism in the Eighteenth Century*, Cambridge University Press, Cambridge, 1970; Ronald Inden, 'Orientalist Constructions of India', in *Modern Asian Studies*, vol. 20, no. 3, 1986, pp. 401–446; Dietmar Rothermund, *The Germany Intellectual Quest for India*, Manohar, New Delhi, 1986; David Kopf, *British Orientalism and the Bengal Renaissance*, University of California Press, 1969; John Drew, *India and the Romantic Imagination*, Oxford University Press, Delhi, 1987.
25. Golwalkar steadfastly rejected the term 'Indian' and refused to accept it as a translation of the commonly accepted Hindi cognate 'Bharatiya'.
26. Gunther-Dietz Sontheimer and Hermann Kulke (eds.), *Hinduism Reconsidered*, Manohar, New Delhi, 1989.
27. Vashudha Dalmia and H von Stietencron (eds.), *Representing Hinduism: The Construction of Religious Traditions and National Identity*, Sage Publications, New Delhi, 1995.
28. Monier-Williams, *Hinduism and its Sources*, Munshiram Manoharlal, New Delhi, 2003, First Indian Edition.
29. For the history of the words 'Hindu' and 'Hinduism', see Chaturvedi Badrinath, *Dharma, India and the World Order*, Saint Andrew Press, Edinburgh, 1993.
30. For an outstanding gloss on the orientalist privileging of Sanskrit over other Indian languages, see G.N. Devy, *After Amnesia*, Orient Longman, Hyderabad, 1990.
31. For a detailed account of this process, see my *Hindutva: Exploring the Idea of Hindu Nationalism*, Penguin Books, New Delhi, 2003.
32. Ibid., pp. 70–123.
33. See an excellent summary in A. Raghuramaraju, *Debates in Indian Philosophy: Classical, Colonial and Contemporary*, Oxford University Press, New Delhi, 2006, pp. 12–13.

34. Ananda K. Coomaraswamy, *Hinduism and Buddhism*, edited by Keshavaram N. Iengar and Rama P. Coomaraswamy, IGNCA and Manohar, New Delhi, 1999 imprint.
35. Ibid., pp. 3–4.
36. K.M. Sen, *Hinduism*, Penguin Books, London, 2005 edition.
37. J.L. Brockington, *The Sacred Thread*, Oxford University Press, New Delhi, 2000 edition.
38. David Kopf, *British Orientalism and the Bengal Renaissance*, pp. 87–89.
39. For the argument in this section, I have depended on two excellent works. Isaiah Berlin, *The Roots of Romanticism*, Chatto & Windus, London, 1999; Noël O'Sullivan, *Fascism*, J.M. Dent & Sons Ltd, London, 1983.
40. Isaiah Berlin, 'Kant as an Unfamiliar Source of Nationalism', in *The Sense of Reality*, Chatto & Windus, London, 1996, p. 247.
41. Fichte's own expression, quoted in Isaiah Berlin, *The Roots of Romanticism*, p. 96.
42. There is little direct evidence of Golwalkar's familiarity with these thinkers first-hand. But these ideas had been absorbed and disseminated in theories of nationalism of that period.
43. Jyotirmaya Sharma, *Hindutva: Exploring the Idea of Hindu Nationalism*, Penguin/Viking, New Delhi, 2003.
44. For a detailed account of Swami Vivekananda's nationalism, see, Jyotirmaya Sharma, *A Restatement of Religion: Swami Vivekananda and the Making of Hindu Nationalism*, Westland/Context, New Delhi, 2019.
45. *Sri Guruji Samagra*, vol. 6, p. 212.
46. *Sri Guruji Samagra*, vol. 7, p. 300.
47. *Sri Guruji Samagra*, vol. 6, pp. 180–1.
48. Christophe Jaffrelot, *The Hindu Nationalist Movement and Indian Politics: 1925 to the 1990s*, Penguin Books, 1999 edition, pp. 53–55.
49. In a conversation with the author in Nagpur in July 2005.
50. For details on the ban on the Sangh see Walter K. Andersen and Sridhar D. Damle, *The Brotherhood in Saffron: The Rashtriya*

Swayamsevak Sangh and Hindu Revivalism, Westview Press, Boulder and London, 1987.

51. *Sri Guruji Samagra*, vol. 2, p. 30.
52. Ibid., p. 31.
53. Ibid., p. 107.
54. *Sri Guruji Samagra*, vol. 9, p. 7.
55. Ibid., p. 7.
56. Arvind Rajagopal, 'Resurrecting Godse: The Hindutva Continuum', *Frontline*, 28 January 1994.
57. Andersen and Damle, p. 43
58. This is based on five letters written by Godse to Savarkar, which are in the author's possession. The contents of these letters were first published in *The Hindu*, 21 September 2004.
59. Letter of 10 July 1938.
60. *The Times of India*, 22 November 1993.
61. Koenraad Elst, *Gandhi and Godse: A Review and A Critique*, Voice of India, New Delhi, 2001, p. 16.
62. Ibid., p. 19.
63. Ibid., p. 17.
64. Ramachandra Guha, 'The Guru of Hate', *The Hindu*, 26 November 2006.
65. Andersen and Damle, p. 48.
66. Rita Kothari, 'RSS in Sindh: 1942–48', *Economic and Political Weekly*, July 8–15, 2006, p. 3011.
67. *Sri Guruji Samagra*, vol. 9, p. 119.
68. *Sri Guruji Samagra*, vol. 6, p. 218.
69. *Sri Guruji Samagra*, vol. 10, p. 5.
70. Ibid., p. 5.
71. Ibid., p. 6.
72. Ibid., p. 6.
73. *Sri Guruji Samagra*, vol. 1, pp. 208–15.
74. *Sri Guruji Samagra*, vol. 1, pp. 215–21.
75. Nathuram Godse, *May It Please Your Honour*, Surya Bharti Prakashan, New Delhi, 2000 edition.

Chapter 1: When Salt Dissolves in Water

1. I have in mind Joseph Brodsky's essays in *Less Than One: Selected Essays,* Penguin Books, Great Britain, 1986. A few of the phrases here are paraphrased from Brodsky's essays here, especially the idea of a stampede, which appears on p. 115 in the essay 'On Tyranny'.
2. Golwalkar defined *dharma* in several ways throughout his life. For him, it variously meant religion, righteousness, limits, a person's designated station and that set of values which elevates and enhances.
3. The story of the founding of the Jan Sangh and its emergence as a political affiliate of the RSS has been told in several excellent commentaries. See Walter K. Andersen and Sridhar D. Damle's *The Brotherhood, in Saffron: The Rashtriya Swayamsevak Sangh and Hindu Revivalism,* Westview Press, Boulder and London, 1987. Also, Christophe Jaffrelot, *The Hindu Nationalist Movement and Indian Politics, 1925 to the 1990s,* Penguin Books, New Delhi, 1999 edition.
4. He quotes a Sanskrit saying, *nripaneeti vaaraanganaiva anekaroopa,* which means that politics is like a woman of the multitude, a harlot, who takes on various guises. In 2004, the current RSS chief, K.S. Sudarshan used the same quote to hit at the BJP, which was in the midst of a leadership crisis after the Lok Sabha election defeat of May 2004.

Chapter 2: We Are Immortality's Children

1. All significant voices who argued in favour of Hindu nationalism attributed India's slavery to its adherence to non-violence. For a detailed account of this, see *Hindutva: Exploring the Idea of Hindu Nationalism,* Penguin Books, New Delhi, 2003.
2. The phrase Golwalkar uses is *atimaanav.* It is safe to assume that Aurobindo was the original inspiration for the use of this term.

3. '*Shrunvantu vishve amritasya putra aa ye dhaamani divyaani tasthuhu*'. Rigveda, 10, 13, 1.
4. The original phrase is in English and was used as part of a lecture to the Sangh in 1960 at Indore.

Chapter 4: Manu's Fish

1. This is Golwalkar's own term and not the author's translation.
2. There is silence on the question of women in Golwalkar except for his vision of women as mothers and the creation of the Bharatmata ideal. For an excellent account of the place of women in the Sangh, see Paola Bacchetta, *Gender in the Hindu Nation: RSS Women as Ideologues*, Women Unlimited, New Delhi, 2004. See my review of the same in *The Hindu*, 24 September 2004.
3. Golwalkar's own phrase in English.

Acknowledgements

This book owes its second life to V.K. Karthika, who enthusiastically agreed to publish this volume again. I owe her a deep debt of gratitude.

I thank Janani Ganesan for all her invaluable help in preparing the book for publication and Saurabh Garge for the cover of the book.

Author's Note

A word about the order of the book. Chapters 1 to 4 are devoted to Golwalkar's thought and are based entirely on the twelve volumes of his collected works. In view of this, the text in these chapters is relatively free of footnotes and citations, except in places where clarifications are required. All translations from Hindi and Marathi into English are by the author.

Index